A Learner Centered Approach To Online Education

A Learner Centered Approach To Online Education

Lisa Harrell

INFORMATION AGE PUBLISHING, INC.
Charlotte, NC • www.infoagepub.com

Library of Congress Cataloging-in-Publication Data

CIP data for this book can be found on the LOC website (loc.gov).

Paperback: 978-1-62396-292-0
Hardcover: 978-1-62396-293-7
E-Book: 978-162396-294-4

Printed in the United States of America

CONTENTS

CHAPTER 1

INTRODUCTION TO ONLINE EDUCATION

This chapter will:

1. Define online education.
2. Describe recent and expected growth in online education.
3. Identify the varied educational needs that can be met through online education.
4. Identify the common fears and concerns educators may have when transitioning to the online environment.
5. Describe the quality of online education.
6. Identify the advantages and disadvantages for the online student.
7. Identify the student competencies needed to promote success in the online environment.
8. Identify the advantages and disadvantages for the online educator.
9. Describe the role of the online educator.
10. Identify the educator competencies needed to promote success in the online environment.

Online education utilizes the Internet for course delivery with the student and educator typically in different locations. Learners communicate electronically with the educator and other learners (Hardy & Bower, 2004; Sims, Dobb, & Hand, 2002). Assignments and assessments are submitted electronically. Educators, instructional designers, and course developers use technology to present course content. Course content can be presented through recorded lectures, slide presentations, text-based documents, interactive online activities of various forms, audio files, video files, pod casts, wikis, live chat sessions, online discussions, live online presentations, video conferencing, and other methods.

Distance education has been utilized for a number of years in higher education. Online education, a form of distance education, has experienced tremendous growth in higher education. Online enrollment was 1.98 million in 2003, 2.35 million in 2004 (Allen & Seaman, 2005), and 3.2 million in 2005 (Allen & Seaman, 2006). Online enrollment increases for 2006–2010 are as follows: 9.7% to 3.5 million in 2006 (Allen & Seaman, 2007); 12.9% to 3.9 million in 2007 (Allen & Seaman, 2008); 17.6% to 4.6 million in 2008 (Allen & Seaman, 2009); 21% to 5.6 million in 2009; (Allen & Seaman, 2010); and 10% to 6.1 million in 2010 (Allen & Seaman, 2011). The increases in online enrollments are significantly greater than overall higher education enrollments with reported growth rates for higher education of: 1.5% in 2006 (Allen & Seaman, 2007); to: 1.2% in 2007 (Allen & Seaman, 2008); to: 1.2% in 2008 (Allen & Seaman, 2009); 2.0% in 2009 (Allen & Seaman, 2010); and 2.0% in 2010 (Allen & Seaman, 2011).

Online and other forms of distance education are also being recognized by K–12 educators as an option to meet the educational needs of students. According to Setzer and Lewis (2005), about 36% of public school systems used online education in 2003 and 72% of those systems planned to expand their online programs. Picciano and Seaman (2007) reported that some form of online learning was provided by the majority of school systems for the 2005–2006 academic year.

Online education is also used to meet other educational needs. Many corporations have implemented online learning to meet training and professional development needs. In a study by Trierweiler and Rivera (2005), participants expected future growth of online learning within their respective businesses. Professionals are utilizing online education to meet continuing education needs. Personal interest classes are also available online which provide opportunities to participate in online courses for almost any topic.

Based on the recent and expected continued growth of online education, more educators will begin to teach online. Some educators will choose to teach courses online while other educators will be encouraged, if not required, to teach courses online. Making the transition from the traditional classroom to the virtual classroom can be an anxiety provoking and overwhelming task even for the experienced educator. Faculty who have not taught online or are relatively new to the online environment may have questions regarding the quality of online education (Gerlich, 2005; Shank, 2005) and the effectiveness of online learning (Kosak et al., 2004). Online educators may be asked by other educators as well as the general public, the question… "How do you *teach* online?".

Faculty new to online education have also expressed other concerns and fears about transitioning to the online environment. The concerns that have been reported include concerns about the amount of time needed to prepare a course for online delivery and concerns about the amount of time it takes to teach online (Gerlich, 2005; Shank, 2005). Shank (2005) identified additional faculty concerns including: some courses cannot be taught online, lack of connection with students, and educator difficulty in learning new software and/or course management systems. Kosak et al., (2004) further indicated that instructors new to online education have concerns about the support provided by the learning institution and the compensation for teaching an online course. Lee and Busch (2005) indicated that faculty may fear adequate training for teaching online will not be made available. Finally, Hollis and Madill (2006), indicated "there is apprehension about difficulties that online situations may present with regard to cheating, maintaining control over the academic process, class sizes, selection of course management systems, intellectual property and copyright, and the distribution of courses as institutional commodities" (p. 66).

This chapter includes information on quality in online education. This chapter also includes information on the student and educator in online education. Finally, this chapter includes information on preparation for online learning.

QUALITY IN ONLINE EDUCATION

The quality of online education is a concern for many educators. However, research has shown that online courses can be as good as or better than traditional courses (Hiltz & Turoff, 2005; Hollis & Madill, 2006). According to Allen and Seaman (2006), 62% of academic leaders indicated that learning outcomes for online education were as good as or better than those in face to face education. Shovein, Houston, Fox, and Damazo (2005) stated "there are no significant differences in learning outcomes for students taught in traditional classrooms compared with distance education technologies" (p. 343).

According to Shank (2005), the overall quality of an online course is based on the design of the course and the quality of teaching, not the method used to deliver the course. Aragon, Johnson, and Shaik (2002) also supported the concept of good instructional design as a determining factor in the quality of an online course and in the facilitation of student learning. Quality online courses should be learner-centered (Parker, 2004) and provide opportunities for interaction, practice, and feedback.

Resources for Quality in Online Education

National Education Association: Guide to Online High School Courses®	This web-site provides information on online high school courses provided by the National Education Association. http://www.nea.org/home/30113.htm
Quality Matters: Inter-Institutional Quality Assurance in Online Learning®	This web-site provides resources and fee-based services addressing quality in online education. www.qualitymatters.org
The Sloan Consortium: A Consortium of Institutions and Organizations Committed to Quality Online Education®	This web-site provides resources addressing quality in online education. http://www.sloan-c.org/

THE STUDENT AND ONLINE EDUCATION

Advantages for the Student

There are numerous student advantages for online learning documented in the literature. The advantages fall into four main categories. The four categories are: flexibility and increased access to resources; increased student engagement; increased student satisfaction; and promotion of lifelong learning.

Increased Flexibility and Increased Access to Resources

Online education provides increased flexibility for course participation (Ally, 2004; Anderson, 2004; Benson et al., 2005, Hiltz & Turoff, 2005; Hirschheim, 2005; Gomory, 2001; Hollis & Madill, 2006; Lee & Busch, 2005; Roblyer, 2006; Setzer & Lewis, 2005; Shovein et al., 2005; Summers, Waigandt, & Whittaker 2005). Students can typically participate in online courses twenty-four hours a day, seven days a week provided assignments are submitted by the due dates given by the course instructor. Thus, many students find online education to be more convenient (Hirschheim, 2005; Hollis & Madill, 2006; Gomory, 2001; Kosak et al., 2004).

Online education provides increased access to learning resources (Ally, 2004; Anderson; 2004; Shovein et al., 2005). Students in remote geographical locations are able to take courses that would otherwise be unavailable (Hardy & Bower, 2004; Hollis & Madill, 2006; Kosak et al., 2004; Maddux, 2004; Mupinga, 2005). Online education allows students to take courses that would otherwise not be available due to personal circumstances (Benson et al., 2005; Hardy & Bower, 2004; Maddux, 2004; Roblyer, 2006). Online education provides more choices to the student through expanded course offerings (Hollis & Madhill, 2006; Pape, 2005; Mupinga, 2005; Roblyer, 2006; Ronsisvalle & Watkins, 2005; Setzer & Lewis, 2005). Online education may also allow high school students opportunities for credit recovery (Roblyer, 2006) and opportunities to take online college level courses.

Increased Student Engagement

Most online courses require students to participate in synchronous and/ or asynchronous discussions. This requirement facilitates student engagement with the course content (Hollis & Madhill, 2006) and increased interaction with the educator and other students in the class (Shovein et al., 2005). Benson et al. (2009) indicated that online education may improve the social skills of students. Students who may not actively participate in a traditional class due to fear or shyness may feel more comfortable participating in an online course (Brown & Corkhill, 2007; Gomory, 2001; Pape, 2005). Finally, students have the "...opportunity for personal and self-directed learning" (Shovein et al., 2005, p. 342) which promotes student engagement.

Increased Student Satisfaction

Student satisfaction can be higher in online courses than traditional courses if the appropriate technology is chosen for course delivery and there is an appropriate level of educator interaction with students (Hollis & Madhill, 2006). Online courses should also have the appropriate level of student–student interaction and student–content interaction. Because online education can be designed to address all learning styles (Pape, 2005), student satisfaction is facilitated.

Promotion of Life-long Learning

Online education can promote life-long learning by developing a learner's independence (Hughes, 2004). Online learning provides opportunities for continuing education throughout one's professional career (Hollis & Madill, 2006). Gomory (2001) indicated that online continuing education allows learners to pursue educational opportunities without missing work. Gomory (2001) also indicated that online education promotes the ability to learn at any stage of life.

Disadvantages for the Student

There are a few disadvantages for the online student. Fear of technology is a common disadvantage for the online student (Hollis & Madill, 2006). Some students may also have concerns about the lack of social interaction or community (Hollis & Madill, 2006). Finally, students may sign up for an online course without possessing the competencies necessary for success in an online course. Interest in online learning does not mean the student will necessarily be successful in an online learning experience (Roblyer & Marshall, 2003).

Student Competencies Needed To Promote Success in the Online Environment

The successful online student possesses several competencies. The student must have access to the specific technology (hardware and software) required for the online course (Hollis & Madill, 2006; Mupinga Nora, & Yaw, 2006; Roblyer & Marshall, 2003). The student should be proficient in the technology required for the online course (Ascough, 2002; Hughes, 2004; Mupinga et al., 2006; Roblyer & Marshall, 2003; Summers et al., 2005). Some technology deficiencies can be taught through a required orientation course.

Other competencies of the successful online student include: awareness of learning style (Hughes, 2004); organizational skills (Maddux, 2004; Roblyer & Marshall, 2003; Summers et al., 2005); time management skills (Ascough, 2002; Maddux, 2004); above average study skills (Roblyer & Marshall, 2003); and the ability to communicate effectively in writing (Mupinga et al., 2006). The student must also be motivated to participate and succeed in the online course environment (Aragon et al., 2002; Ascough, 2002; Lee & Bush, 2005; Roblyer & Marshall, 2003; Ronsisvalle & Watkins, 2005; Summers et al., 2005). The successful online student will also have a positive attitude toward the course and the online educational process (Roblyer & Marshall, 2003). In addition, the successful online student must be self directed and take responsibility for his/her own learning (Maddux, 2004; Roblyer & Marshall 2003; Ronsisvalle & Watkins, 2005; Summers et al., 2005).

During the advising and registration process, students should be informed that online classes are not easier than on campus classes and are usually more time consuming than traditional on campus courses (Ascough, 2002; Yoon, 2003). Many students are not aware of the time commitment needed for an online course prior to signing up for an online course. Even if the student possess all the competencies for participation in an online course, knowledge of expected time requirements and commitments can assist the student in making an informed decision about enrolling in an online course.

THE EDUCATOR AND ONLINE EDUCATION

Advantages for the Educator

Online education offers several advantages to the online educator. Online education bundles course materials together (Hiltz & Turoff, 2005). Once the online course is developed and organized, updates and revisions can be easily made (Pape, 2005). Online education also allows the educator to increase student access to a variety of learning materials using multiple types of media (Anderson, 2004).

There are other advantages for the online educator. Properly designed courses can foster interaction with the educator, other students, and the content through asynchronous and synchronous methods. In asynchronous communication methods, students and teachers have more time to think about the content before responding to questions, thereby promoting a deeper exploration of the subject matter (Shovein et al., 2005).

Disadvantages for the Educator

There are also disadvantages for the online educator. The educator may be required to teach online without adequate preparation and training (Bower, 2001; Cuellar, 2002; Hollis & Madhill; 2006; Maddux, 2004; Pape, 2002). Online education requires a different approach to course development; course design; educator roles; learning and teaching activities; and assessment activities than traditional education (Maddux, 2004). Some educators may not wish to or be able to change their approach to teaching in order to teach an online course (Shovein et al., 2005).

The educator may not have time allocated for course development (Bower, 2001; Hollis & Madhill, 2006) and/or management. Online course development, preparation, and management are more time consuming than traditional courses (Bower, 2001; Hardy & Bower, 2004; Hollis & Madhill, 2006; Kosak et al., 2004; Maddux, 2004; Lee & Bush, 2005; Pape, 2005; Shovein et al., 2005; Sieber, 2005). According to Pape (2005), "it is critical that teachers play a daily role in online classes—guiding students in their learning experiences, providing timely and appropriate feedback, moderating and facilitating in-depth discussions, and modifying course delivery and assessment to meet a variety of learning styles" (p. 15).

Role of the Online Educator

In the online course, the educator assumes the role of course facilitator, mentor, and moderator (Anderson, 2004; Hardy & Bower, 2004; Parker, 2004; Shovein et al., 2005; Sieber, 2005). The online educator may also be required to design and develop the course, or the institution may have a team including a content expert, the educator, a course designer, and a course developer that designs and develops the course. In all cases, the online educator should promote active learning (Sieber, 2005).

Educator Competencies Needed to Promote Success in the Online Environment

The successful online educator possesses several competencies. The educator must be motivated to participate in the online course (Roblyer & Marshall, 2003), have a commitment to teaching and learning (Williams, 2003), and be a content expert in the subject matter for the online course (Summers et al., 2005; Williams, 2003). The online educator must also be organized, be able to set goals, have good time management skills (Roblyer & Marshall, 2003), and possess effective communication skills (Hollis & Madhill, 2006; Kosak et al., 2004).

The successful online educator must be knowledgeable in educational theory and practice, instructional design principles, and possess good research skills (Williams, 2003). Furthermore, the educator must be knowledgeable in online teaching strategies and methods (Hardy & Bower, 2004; Hiltz & Turoof, 2005; Kosak et al., 2004; Summers et al., 2005; Williams, 2003). It also recommended that educators participate in an online course as a student prior to becoming an online educator. Prior experience with online learning as a student, promotes educator success in the online environment (Roblyer & Marshall, 2003).

Additional competencies are also needed. The educator must be proficient in the use of the technology required for the course (Ascough 2002; Kosak et al., 2004; Lee & Bush, 2005; Roblyer & Marshall, 2003; Sieber, 2005). Finally, the educator must be familiar with accessibility issues and copy right issues (Ascough, 2002).

In preparing to teach or learn online, it is important that competencies are assessed either formally or informally through self-assessment. If the needed competencies have not been achieved, the deficient areas should be addressed prior to participating on an online course. This is a crucial step toward success.

PREPARATION FOR ONLINE LEARNING

Students and educators who possess the competencies to be successful in the online environment also need adequate preparation for their online learning experience (Hughes, 2004; Mupinga 2005; Roblyer, 2006). Teaching in the online environment is much different than teaching in the traditional classroom. Engaging students through active learning is an important component of quality online instruction (Kosak et al., 2006). For many educators this may be very different from traditional methods of teaching (Caplan, 2004; Kosak et al., 2006).

Online readiness quizzes can be helpful in preparing to learn or teach online. It is recommended that institutions require online readiness quizzes for all students and educators interested in participating in an online learning experience. Hollis and Madill (2006), indicated there is a "…need to access student readiness and their attitude towards learning" (p. 66). Hughes (2004) indicated that assessing a learner's readiness for online learning increases their chances for success.

CONCLUSION

There are several important issues regarding online education addressed in this chapter. Online education is used for many educational purposes. Online education has experienced recent growth and this growth is expected to continue. Online education can be as effective as or more effective than traditional courses. There are advantages and disadvantages for the online student and the online educator. There are specific competencies online students and online educators need to possess in order to be successful in the online learning environment. The online student and online educator must be adequately prepared for the online learning experience.

CHAPTER 1 APPLICATION EXERCISE

This application exercise will allow you to reflect on and evaluate competencies, weaknesses, and preparedness in regards to online education.

1. What did you learn about your preparedness to teach online?

2. What specific competencies do you have that will help you be a successful online teacher?

3. What are the areas of weakness you will need to improve upon in order to become a successful online teacher?

REFERENCES

Allen, I. E., & Seaman, J. (2005). Growing by degrees: Online education in the United States, 2005. *The Sloan Consortium.* Retrieved from http://www.sloan-c. org/publications/survey/pdf/growing_by_degrees.pdf

Allen, I. E., & Seaman, J. (2006). Making the grade: Online education in the United States, 2006. *The Sloan Consortium.* Retrieved from http://sloanconsortium. org/sites/default/files/Making_the_Grade.pdf

Allen, I. E., & Seaman, J. (2007). Online nation: Five years of growth in online learning. *The Sloan Consortium.* Retrieved from http://www.sloan-c.org/publications/survey/pdf/online_nation.pdf

Allen, I. E., & Seaman, J. (2008). Staying the course: Online education in the United States, 2008. *The Sloan Consortium.* Retrieved from http://sloanconsortium.org/sites/default/files/staying_the_course-2.pdf

Allen, I. E., & Seaman, J. (2009). Learning on demand: Online education in the United States, 2009. *The Sloan Consortium.* Retrieved from http://sloanconsortium.org/publications/survey/pdf/learningondemand.pdf

Allen, I. E., & Seaman, J. (2010). Class differences: Online education in the United States, 2010. *The Sloan Consortium.* Retrieved from http://sloanconsortium.org/publications/survey/class_differences

Allen, I. E., & Seaman, J. (2011). Going the distance. Online education in the United States, 2011. *The Sloan Consortium.* Retrieved from http://www.onlinelearningsurvey.com/reports/goingthedistance.pdf

Ally, M. (2004). Foundations of educational theory for online learning: In T. Anderson & F. Elloumi (Eds.), *Theory and practice of online learning* (pp. 3–31). Retrieved from http://cde.athabascauca/online_book/pdf/TPOL_chp01.pdf

Anderson, T. (2004). Teaching in an online learning context: In T. Anderson & F. Elloumi (Eds.), *Theory and practice of online learning* (pp. 273–294). Retrieved from http://cde.athabascau.ca/online_book/pdf/TPOL_chp11.pdf

Aragon, S. R., Johnson, S. D., & Shaik, N. (2002). The influence of learning style preferences on student success in online versus face-to-face environments. *The American Journal of Distance Education, 16*(4), 227–244.

Ascough, R. S. (2002). Designing for online education: Putting pedagogy before technology. *Teaching Theology and Religion, 5*(1), 17–29.

Benson, A. D., Johnson, S. D., Taylor, G. D., Treat, T., Shinkareva, O. N., & Duncan, J. (2005). Achievement in online and campus-based career and technical education (CTE) courses. *Community College Journal of Research and Practice, 29,* 369–394.

Bower, B. L. (2001). Distance education: Facing the faculty challenge. *Online Journal of Distance Learning Administration, IV*(II). Retrieved from http://www.westga.edu/~distance/ojdla/summer42/bower42.html

Brown, W., & Corkill, P. (2007). Postsecondary online education. *Education Digest, 73*(1), 39–42.

Caplan, D. (2004). The development of online courses. In T. Anderson & F. Elloumi (Eds.), *Theory and practice of online learning* (pp. 175–194). Retrieved from http://cde.athabascau.ca/online_book/pdf/TPOL_chp07.pdf

Cuellar, N. (2002). The transition from classroom to online teaching. *Nursing Forum, 37*(3), 5–13.

Gerlich, R. N. (2005). Faculty perceptions of distance learning. *Distance Education Report, 9*(17), 8.

Gomory, R. (2001). Internet learning: Is it real and what does it mean for universities? *Journal of Asynchronous Learning Networks, 5*(1), 139–146. Retrieved from www.aln.org/publications/jaln/v5n1/v5n1_gomory.asp

Hardy, K. P., & Bower, B. L. (2004). Instructional and work life issues for distance learning faculty. *New Directions for Community Colleges, 128,* 47–54.

Hiltz, S. R., & Turoff, M. (2005). Education goes digital: The evolution of online learning and the revolution in higher education. *Communications of the ACM, 48*(10), 59–64.

Hirschheim, R. (2005). The internet-based education band wagon: Look before you leap. *Communications of the ACM, 48*(7), 97–101.

Hollis, V., & Madill, H. (2006). Online learning: The potential for occupational therapy education. *Occupational Therapy Int., 13*(2), 61–78.

Hughes, J. (2004). Supporting the online learner. In T. Anderson & F. Elloumi (Eds.), *Theory and practice of online learning* (pp. 367–384). Retrieved from http://cde.athabascau.ca/online_book/pdf/TPOL_chp15.pdf

Kosak, L., Manning, D., Dobson, E., Rogerson, L., Cotnam, S., Colaric, S., & McFadden, C. (2004). Prepared to teach online? Perspectives of faculty in the university of North Carolina system. *Online Journal of Distance Learning Administration, VII*(III), 1–13. Retrieved from http://www.westga.edu/%7Edistance/ojdla/fall73/kosak73.html

Lee, J. A., & Bush, P. E. (2005). Factor's related to instructor's willingness to participate in distance education. *The Journal of Educational Research, 99*(2), 109–115.

Maddux, C. D. (2004). Developing online courses: Ten myths. *Rural Special Education Quarterly, 23*(2), 27–32.

Mupinga, D. M. (2005). Distance education in high schools. *Clearing House, January/February, 78*(3), 105–108.

Mupinga, D. M., Nora, R. T., & Yaw, D. C. (2006). The learning styles, expectations, and needs of online students. *College Teaching, 54*(1), 185–189.

Pape, L. (2005). High school on the WEB. *American School Board Journal, 192*(7), 12–16.

Parker, N. K. (2004). The quality dilemma in online education: In T. Anderson & F. Elloumi (Eds.), *Theory and practice of online learning* (385–421). Retrieved from http://cde.athabascau.ca/online_book/pdf/TPOL_chp16.pdf

Picciano, A., & Seaman, J. (2007). K–12 online learning a survey of U.S. school district administrators. *The Sloan Consortium.* Retrieved from http://sloanconsortium.org/sites/default/files/K–12_Online_Learning_1.pdf

Roblyer, M. D. (2006). Online high-school programs that work. *Education Digest, 72*(3), 55–63.

Roblyer, M. D., & Marshall, J. C. (2003). Predicting success of virtual high school students: Preliminary results from an educational success prediction instrument. Journal *of Research on Technology in Education, 35*(2), 241–255.

Ronsisvalle, T., & Watkins, R. (2005). Student success in online K–12 education. *The Quarterly Review of Distance Education, 6*(2), 117–124.

Setzer, J. C., & Lewis, L. (2005). Distance education courses for public elementary and secondary school students: 2002–03. *Education Statistics Quarterly, 7*(1/2). Retrieved from http://nces.edgov/programs/quarterly/vol_7/1_2/4_5.asp

Shank, P. S. (2005). 5 common fears about teaching online-fact vs. fiction. *Distance Education Report, 9*(24), 5–7.

Shovein, J., Huston, C., Fox, S., & Damazo, B. (2005). Challenging traditional teaching and learning paradigms: Online learning and emancipatory teaching. *Nursing Education Perspectives, 26*(6), 340–343.

Sieber, J. C. (2005). Misconceptions and realities about teaching online. *Science and Engineering Ethics, 11*, 329–340.

Sims, R., Dobbs, G., & Hand, T. (2002). Enhancing quality in online learning: Scaffolding planning and design through proactive evaluation. *Distance Education, 23*(2), 135–148.

Summers, J. J., Waigandt, A, & Whittaker, T. A. (2005). A comparison of student achievement and satisfaction in an online versus a traditional face-to-face statistics class. *Innovative Higher Education, 29*(3), 233–250.

Trierweiler, C., & Rivera, R. (2005). Is online higher education right for corporate learning? *Training and Development, 59*(9), 44–47.

Williams, P. E. (2003). The roles and competencies for distance education programs in higher education. *The American Journal of Distance Education, 17*(1), 45–57.

Yoon, S. (2003). In search of meaningful online learning experiences. *New Directions for Adult and Continuing Education, 100*, 19–30.

CHAPTER 2

RESOURCES AND SUPPORT FOR THE ONLINE STUDENT AND EDUCATOR

This chapter will:

1. Identify the benefits of a student online orientation course.
2. Identify the benefits of an educator online orientation course.
3. Identify types of tutorials that can be included in a student online orientation course.
4. Identify types of tutorials that can be included in an educator online orientation course.
5. Identify the different types of academic support and the significance of each to the online student and educator.
6. Identify the different types of resources online students and educators need access to and the significance of each in the online environment.
7. Describe the importance of technical support in the online environment.

A Learner Centered Approach To Online Education, pages 13–28.
Copyright © 2013 by Information Age Publishing
All rights of reproduction in any form reserved.

8. Identify the benefits of mentoring for the online student and educator.
9. Identify and describe the components of a course management system.
10. Describe the difference between commercial, open source, and home grown course management systems.

Resources and support for the online student and educator are crucial for successful online programs. This chapter includes information on the following topics: student orientation course and tutorials; educator orientation course; and support systems. This chapter also includes information on course management systems.

STUDENT ORIENTATION
COURSE AND TUTORIALS

Even though a student may possess the competencies needed to be successful in the online environment, more preparation is needed prior to participating in an online course. The student may enter an online course with little or no online course experience, with a less than optimal level of understanding of how to navigate the course management system, and without an understanding of the expectations, guidelines, and requirements of an online course. Students who experience these types of issues may become frustrated and may also withdraw from the course due to these technical issues that are not related to the content of the course. Requiring students to pass an online orientation course that addresses these and other important areas, prior to registration in an online course, will increase the student's likelihood of succeeding in the online environment.

Clerehan, Turnbull, Moore, Brown, and Tuovinen (2003) supported the use of online course orientations and further indicated that tutorials increase student engagement and interaction. Scagnoli (2001) stated, "orientation for online courses serve the same objectives as orientation for college, in that it can facilitate academic and social interactions, increase students involvement, enhance the sense of belonging to a virtual learning community, and help retention" (p. 20). In a study by Lynch (2001), students who completed a required orientation course showed significant increases in technology skills, self-directed learning, and online communication skills.

During the orientation course, students will become familiar with the instructional media used in online courses and practice using the technology such as communication tools. This will increase the likelihood of success. Orientation courses and tutorials promote student accountability as the student has been made aware of expectations and has been given access to the information and tools needed for success. Student retention can also be increased by providing online orientations and tutorials (Lynch, 2001).

There are a variety of tutorials and other important information that can be included in the orientation course to promote student success and retention. The tutorials and information should also be made available across all online courses. Each institution/educator should determine which tutorials and/or information are appropriate to include. Several examples of tutorials will now be presented.

Competencies Needed to Be Successful in an Online Course

A student should be aware of the competencies needed to be successful in an online course by the time he/she has enrolled in the orientation course, but it can be helpful to reinforce the competencies needed for success. This can be done though various methods. One simple method is to include an online self-assessment quiz that the institution or educator develops or provide the link to a resource that the institution has approved for use.

Navigating the Course Management System

Specific step by step instructions should be provided on how to navigate the course management system. Each online course should also include information on navigation that is specific for that course. A navigation tutorial can be done in a variety of methods. One recommendation is to use screen recording software to record and narrate a step by step video of course navigation.

Writing Basics and Plagiarism

All online courses will include some type of writing assignments. Students will enter a course with varied experience and expertise in writing. Therefore, tutorials should be included on writing basics for all courses. Information on the required referencing format should be included in the writing tutorial. Plagiarism is very important to address as part of the writing tutorial. The specific institution's policy on plagiarism should be included as well as information on what constitutes plagiarism. Many institutions may also require that assignments be sent to a plagiarism detection service. If this is required, the writing tutorial should include information on how to access and utilize the plagiarism detection service. The writing tutorial should also include information on institution specific resources including online writing centers.

Resources on Writing and Plagiarism

Purdue Online Writing Lab®	The Online Writing Lab (OWL) ® at Purdue University provides information on a variety of topics related to writing. The resources are free for noncommercial purposes including personal, education, and training. If linking to the site, it is requested that users notify the coordinator. http://owl.english.purdue.edu/owl/
Plagiarism. org®	Plagiarism.org® provides information on plagiarism and how to prevent plagiarism. Links to detection tools are also provided. http://www.plagiarism.org/index.html
Turnitin.com®	Turnitin.com® is a plagiarism detection tool from iParadigms, LLC available to institutions for a fee. In addition to plagiarism detection, Turnitin® also provides GradeMark® and PeerMark® resources. There are building blocks available for various course management systems that allow Turnitin® to be integrated within the course management system the institution is using. https://turnitin.com/static/index.php
WriteCheck™	WriteCheck™ is a writing resource available to students which provides the opportunity for students to purchase credits to submit papers for plagiarism detection, grammar check, and spelling check prior to submitting papers for grading in courses. https://www.writecheck.com/static/home.html

Using the Course E-mail in the Course Management System

Although educators typically have an e-mail associated with their institution, it is recommended that educators use the course e-mail within the course management system for each online course if this tool is available. This will keep all communications for a course contained within that course. This practice will help with course management as students often do not indicate the course for which their question(s) is related to when sending communications. If an educator is teaching multiple courses, it is time consuming to go to the rosters and find the student's course in order for the question to be properly addressed. Using course e-mail also helps to ensure that communications are only being viewed by the student. Student's personal e-mail accounts may be family/group accounts that can be accessed by others. This is especially important if sending feedback for grading and other sensitive issues. If a course specific e-mail is not available, educators should use the institution provided e-mail address for the student.

Accessing and Submitting Assignments

Course management systems utilize various methods for submitting assignments. It is recommended that educators set up assignments to be submitted to an assignment specific drop box as opposed to being sent to a general drop box. Students should be given a step by step tutorial on how to use the technology needed for assignment completion and how to submit various types of assignments including discussions. Using screen recording software or screen capture software is very helpful for this type of tutorial.

Participating in Online Discussion Boards

Discussion boards are available within the course management system. Students submit their initial postings and reply to other students and the instructor for each posted topic. Discussing a topic in an online course differs from the discussion that occurs in a traditional classroom. It is expected that discussion board postings be well thought out and reflective. Students should use correct grammar and spelling. Many educators have length requirements and/or quantity requirements for discussion board postings. Depending on the program or course, the educator may also require the use of references. Educators should provide students with the information needed to successfully participate in online discussion boards.

Using Online Libraries and Data Bases

Most institutions now have online libraries and/or other online data bases to assist students with their research needs. It is important that students know how to access these resources and how to use them. The tutorials should provide the link to these resources and how to obtain passwords if needed, as well as other pertinent information.

Understanding Grading Rubrics

Rubrics should be provided for all writing assignments. However, students may not refer to the rubrics as assignments are completed. Students who do refer to the rubrics may not understand how to read and understand the rubrics. Providing a grading rubric tutorial can assist students in these areas.

Policies on Feedback from Educators

Individual institutions may have a required policy regarding feedback from educators. Individual institutions may allow educators to develop their own policies. At a minimum, these policies should include: response time for e-mail, phone messages, discussion board postings, and grading.

The policies should also include the procedure for notifying students if the educator will be unavailable.

Evaluating Information Found on the Internet

Students use the Internet for a significant amount of research to complete their course work. It is important that students know what type of online resources are appropriate and how to evaluate resources. A tutorial in this area can assist students in finding appropriate resources.

Resources on Evaluating Information Found on the Internet

Purdue Online Writing Lab®	The Online Writing Lab (OWL) ® at Purdue University provides information on a variety of topics related to writing. The resources are free for noncommercial purposes including personal, education, and training. If linking to the site, it is requested that users notify the coordinator. http://owl.english.purdue.edu/owl/
UC Berkeley Library®	This link is for the UC Berkeley Library's "Evaluating Web Pages"®. This resource provides a variety of information on this topic. There are also links to other resources. http://www.lib.berkeley.edu/TeachingLib/Guides/Internet/Evaluate.html

Tips for Success for the Online Student

It is important that students are aware of strategies that will help improve the likelihood of success in the online environment. A very important strategy for success is to log into the course and check e-mail regularly, at least every other day. There are other tips and strategies that should be included like planning time for course work, planning quality study time, developing time management skills, and how to get help.

Netiquette

The rules for communicating online may not be clear to the new online student. It is important that students be aware of appropriate communication guidelines in the online environment, what constitutes inappropriate and unacceptable communication, privacy issues, and other important factors in regards to communicating in the online environment. Institutions may have these policies in place or the individual educator may have to develop his/her own.

In addition to the student benefits of tutorials, there are educator benefits as well. By providing tutorials, the educator's time can be focused on the content of the course. Educators may be able to simply refer students to the tutorial that addresses the non-content related question. Tutorials can be time consuming to develop, but many tutorials can be used for multiple courses. If the institution does not have an orientation course, individual educators should develop tutorials that can be used across multiple courses as well as the tutorials specific to the individual course. It is recommended that educators at each institution work together to develop tutorials that can be used across multiple courses and share those resources across courses. The individual educator can then develop the tutorials specific to his/her course(s).

EDUCATOR ORIENTATION COURSE

It is also recommend that a new online educator be required to complete an online orientation and training course similar in set up to the course he/she will be teaching. This allows the educator to experience an online course from a student perspective while helping the educator achieve the competencies needed to be successful in the online environment. Caplan (2004) indicated being a student in an online course allows "...teachers to experience the same challenges that their students will face: problems with inadequate computer abilities, learning about the variety of interactive tools, and underestimating the amount of time needed to complete online readings and homework" (p. 183). It also allows the educator to see how the facilitator of the training course interacts and participates in the course (Ascough, 2002).

As part of the online orientation and training course, the new online educator should be given a course shell in the course management system to begin course development or exploration (if the course has been previously developed) with guidance from a facilitator. The online orientation and training course should include all the tutorials and other information that are a part of the student orientation course. The online orientation and training course should also include tutorials and information on: interaction with students; online course design and development; general technology tools for teaching online; teaching strategies appropriate for online learning; factors affecting student participation/motivation; copyright issues; accessibility issues; minimum log in and contact requirements; policies regarding grading and feedback; and others as deemed appropriate by the institution.

Both student and educator orientation courses should also require participants to submit sample assignments (Roblyer, 2006). This can include sample discussions, practice sending attachments, writing samples, etc. The tutorials and information included in the orientation should be designed to meet the needs of the learners and the online program.

SUPPORT SYSTEMS

The next step in promoting success in the online environment is ensuring adequate support systems. Support for the online student and educator is crucial to success. Adequate support can promote student success (Wheeler, 2006), retention (Jorgensen, 2004; Smith & Curry, 2005), and satisfaction (Jorgensen, 2004). The support systems necessary for online education fall into four categories: academic support, access to resources, technical support, and mentoring.

Academic Support

Program Information
It is important for institutions providing online education to have policies and procedures in place for notifying students of how to log in, the date they can access the course, and the last date they will be allowed to first access the course once the course starts. Students should also be provided with the contact information for technical support. Institutions can use a variety of methods to get this information to students. The information can be provided through letters given at the time of registration, mailed through the postal service, or e-mailed.

Online Student and Online Educator Manuals
The policies and expectations for online students and educators can be very different from those in traditional education. Both students and educators should have a manual that clearly outlines all policies and procedures for the institution. Instructions and policies should be clear (Hughes, 2004; Scagnoli, 2001) and consistent throughout the institution (Smith & Curry, 2005). The manual should be a part of the required orientation course for both students and educators and should also be linked within all online courses. An institution's student handbook often includes valuable information regarding the institution's specific policies. These policies address such issues as attendance, course withdrawal, academic dishonesty, student rights, student responsibilities, grade appeals, and others. The student handbook should also include contact information for all personnel an online student may need to contact.

Advisors/Counselors
The need for advisors and counselors is supported in the literature (Hughes, 2004; Smith & Curry, 2005). This is an important component of

any online program for both students and educators. Advisors and counselors can assist educators by assisting with students who have poor academic performance; those not participating or submitting assignments; and those with other personal and academic issues. Advisors and counselors can also assist with issues related to student disabilities.

Study Skills Assistance/Tutoring

Study skills assistance and tutoring can be very beneficial to the online student. Study skills assistance can include such topics as time management, test taking, reading comprehension, writing, referencing, library resources, and evaluating online information (Hughes, 2004). These topics can also be addressed through course tutorials. Tutoring services can be beneficial to the student needing assistance with mastering course content.

Online Coordinator

Online education programs should have a designated online coordinator (Roblyer, 2006). The responsibilities of the online coordinator can include assigning user names and passwords; setting up course shells for new courses; maintaining the database of archived courses; populating courses with instructors and students; assisting with educating instructors and students in the use of the course management system; and performing other tasks related to the course management system. Another important function of the online coordinator is to assist advisors and others in ensuring students receive the proper preparation and acquire the necessary competencies needed to be successful in the online environment prior to enrolling in an online course. The online coordinator should take an active role in developing student and educator resources to promote success in the online environment.

Addressing Students with Disabilities

Students with disabilities may need special consideration in the online course such as accommodations for timed tests and assignments, alternate methods of learning (Hughes, 2004), and others. Students may have visual, hearing, mobility, and/or special learning needs that require accommodations. Institutions should have policies and procedures in place for assisting and accommodating students with disabilities.

Online Course Evaluation

Course and instructor evaluation is an important component of an online course (Smith & Curry 2005). The information that is obtained through course evaluation will be important in identifying professional development needs for instructors and other issues that need to be addressed to facilitate student learning in the online course. Student, course, and instructor evaluations should be set up so that submission is anonymous.

Documented Student Rights and Responsibilities

Online students should be provided with documented student rights and responsibilities and the code of conduct for the institution (Hughes, 2004). Academic integrity policies should be included in the online course. The policies should include the consequences for a violation of the academic integrity policy. Student rights and responsibilities, the code of conduct, and the academic integrity policy should be included in the online student and educator handbook. It is also helpful to include these policies within the syllabus for each course.

Learning Agreements

Smith and Curry (2005) recommended that learners be provided with a learning agreement prior to starting an online course. A learning agreement "can help to set out what is expected from online distance learners, what they can expect from the institution and what to do if things go wrong" (Smith & Curry, p. 397). Learning agreements can be submitted electronically within the course management system.

Access to Resources

Access to Online Libraries and Library Support

Online students and educators should have equivalent access to library resources and support as the traditional classroom participants (Smith & Curry, 2005). It is recommended that online educators and students have access to digital libraries (Hughes, 2004) and data bases. Students and educators should be provided with information regarding the proper procedures for accessing library resources and any materials available.

Access to Software and Hardware

Students should be made aware of any software and hardware requirements prior to enrolling in a course. Students should be provided with links to web-sites for downloads of free software needed for viewing and accessing course materials. For example, if an educator posts Power Point® slide presentations for students to view but the student does not have access to this software, the student can download the free Power Point® Viewer to view the presentations.

Access to Computers and Reliable High Speed Internet Connection

Students and educators should have adequate access to a computer and a reliable high speed Internet connection prior to enrolling in an online course. Many of the technologies used in online education are not compatible with dial up Internet access. Most institutions have computer labs that can be accessed by online students. Public libraries also have computer and Internet access. However, it is recommended that an online student and educator have a personal computer and Internet connection in order to access the course(s) without having to plan course participation around the operating hours of the institution or library.

Technical Support (Help Desk)

A help desk is crucial for the resolution of student and educator technical issues (Hughes, 2004; Maddux, 2004). Students and educators should receive prompt assistance with any technical issues. Lack of prompt attention in this area can lead to participant frustration (Wheeler, 2006). The help desk should provide: technical support (Ascough, 2002; Roblyer & Marshall, 2003; Smith & Curry, 2005), assistance with downloading files (Wheeler 2006), password assistance (Wheeler 2006), and other assistance with other technical issues.

Mentoring for the New Online Student and Educator

Mentoring for the new online student can be a tool for promoting success and retention. An experienced student who has been successful in the online environment can offer support to the new online student. Support can be offered in the form of sharing strategies for success, time management tips, and other forms.

It is important for the online educator to have a mentor at least during the first one to two sessions of teaching a course online. Campbell and Campbell (1997) defined mentoring as "a situation in which a more-experienced member of an organization maintains a relationship with a less experienced, often new member to the organization and provides information, support, and guidance, so as to enhance the less-experienced member's chances of success in the organization and beyond" (p. 727). The mentor for the new online educator should be an experienced online educator. The mentor should assist in monitoring and supporting the new online educator (Roblyer, 2006).

Another form of mentoring for the new online educator can occur in the form of a faculty forum. A faculty forum for online educators can be designed and offered within the course management system. The faculty forum will assist online educators in developing community among their peers through interaction. The faculty forum will allow faculty to collaborate on issues, problems, successes, and best practices (Santovec, 2005).

COURSE MANAGEMENT SYSTEMS

Most institutions use course management systems, also known as learning management systems, for the delivery and management of online courses. In addition to use for online courses, course management systems are used to support traditional courses as well as blended or hybrid courses, which are a combination of traditional and online components (Hall, 2003). Course management systems can also be used to provide a delivery mechanism for self-paced online tutorials (Hall, 2003).

Morgan (2003) defined a course management system as "a software system that is specifically designed and marketed for faculty and students to use in teaching and learning" (p. 2). Collis and De Boer (2004) defined a course management system as "a comprehensive software package that supports some or all aspects of course preparation, delivery, communication, participation and interaction and allows these aspects to be available via a network" (p.7). Ullman and Rabinowitz (2004) defined a course management system as "internet based software that manages student enrollment, tracks student performance, and creates and distributes course content" (p. 1).

It is crucial that online educators, as well as students become familiar with the course management system used by the institution. Optimally, the institution will provide formal training in the use of the course management system through an online orientation and training course. If in-house training is not provided, educators should seek training through another source. Educators can also seek guidance from other online instructors who are willing to help those new to online education learn about the course management system.

A great way to become familiar with the course management system and online education is to begin adding online components to traditional courses. Next, the course would progress to a hybrid or blended course. This process can be helpful as educators design and develop an online course.

Components of a Course Management System

Course Organizational Tools

There are several tools the educator can use to organize an online course. Typically, there is a syllabus tool and a calendar tool. There is also some method to organize the content and assignments of the course. On-line courses are typically organized into modules or units through the use of folders or other organizational methods.

Content Delivery Tools

Course management systems provide mechanisms for the delivery of course content materials. Course content and materials can be delivered through the course management system by importing any combination of: audio files: video files; pod casts; presentations; text-based documents; animations; simulations; interactive activities; links to web-sites and electronic resources; SCORM (Sharable Content Object Reference Model); online lessons; learning objects; and others.

Collaboration Tools

Course management systems provide mechanisms for collaboration and communication within the course. Asynchronous (communication between participants does not occur at the same time) collaboration and communication tools include: discussions; e-mail; instructor announcements; wikis; blogs; student home pages; and others. Synchronous (communication between participants occurs at the same time) collaboration and communication tools include: chats, virtual classroom (video conferencing), and instant messaging.

Course Management Tools

Course management systems provide mechanisms for managing the online course. The educator can enroll users in the course, assign user roles, and make the course available or unavailable to users. All assignments can be graded utilizing some form of electronic grading. The grade book is also electronic. The educator can assign groups within the course. The educator can also access statistical information such as student log in data, last access dates, areas of the course the student has accessed, and more. Some course management systems provide more detailed statistical information than others.

Course management systems provide some mechanism for importing and exporting courses. Content and exams from text book publishers can be imported through course cartridges if available. Other course content can be imported through the import function. Exporting courses allows the educator to save a copy of the most recent version of a course. It also provides a zip package that can be imported into another course. Individual institutions may not grant exporting capabilities to educators.

Course management systems also provide some method to copy, archive (backup), and reset courses. Course copy functions allow an educator to copy all course content into a new course shell for the next offering, as opposed to copying the content piece by piece. Archiving or backing up courses is extremely important for documentation and auditing purposes. An archived course includes all the user and student data including assignments and grades. A resetting function allows an educator to reset the course for the next offering once the course has been archived. The reset function may not be available in all course management systems and/or individual institutions may not grant that capability to educators.

Assessment Tools

Course management systems provide methods for assessment in the forms of tests, quizzes, and exams. The questions for tests, quizzes, and exams may be in the form of multiple choice, fill in the blank, essay/discussion, matching, ordering, labeling, and others. Surveys are also a type of assessment tool that can be included in the online course. The course evaluation is typically in the form of a survey.

Types of Course Management Systems

Commercial Course Management Systems

Commercial course management systems require licensing fees for the use of the software. Institutions can either host the course management system or pay to have the system hosted. Commonly utilized commercial course management systems include Blackboard® and Desire2Learn®. There are other commercial management systems available.

Open Source Course Management Systems

Open source course management systems do not require licensing fees for the use of the software. Institutions can either host the course management system or pay to have the system hosted off-site. Commonly utilized open source course management systems include Moodle® and Sakai®. There are other open source course management systems available.

Home Grown Course Management Systems

Home grown course management systems are developed by an individual institution or group of institutions. All aspects of the course management systems are handled in house including development costs, security issues, technical issues, and others. These are the least frequently used type of course management system.

CONCLUSION

Resources and support for the online student and educator are crucial for successful online programs. Student and educator orientations and tutorials are an important resource and means of support. Academic support, access to resources, technical support (help desk), mentoring for the new online student and educator, and the course management system are also important for successful online programs.

CHAPTER 2 APPLICATION EXERCISE

Identify three (3) online course tutorials that you think are the most important tutorials to include in an online course in your specific content area.

REFERENCES

Ascough, R. S. (2002). Designing for online education: Putting pedagogy before technology. *Teaching Theology and Religion, 5*(1), 17–29.

Campbell. T. A., & Campbell, D. E. (1997). Faculty/student mentor program: Effects on academic performance and retention. *Research in Higher Education, 38*(6), 727–742.

Caplan, D. (2004). The development of online courses. In T. Anderson & F. Elloumi (Eds.), *Theory and practice of online learning* (pp. 175–194). Retrieved from http://cde.athabascau.ca/online_book/pdf/TPOL_chp07.pdf

Clerehan, R., Turnbull, J., Moore, T., Brown, A., & Tuovinen, J. (2003). Transforming learner support: An online resource centre for a diverse student population. *Educational Media International, 40,* 15–31.

Collis, B., & De Boer, W. (2004). Teachers as learners: Embedded tools for implementing a CMS. *TechTrends: Linking Research & Practice to Improve Learning, 48*(6), 7–12.

Hall, J. (2003). *Assessing learning management systems.* Retrieved from http://www.clomedia.com/content/templates/clo_feature.asp?articleid=91&zoneid=29

Hughes, J. (2004). Supporting the online learner. In T. Anderson & F. Elloumi (Eds.), *Theory and practice of online learning* (pp. 367–384). Retrieved from http://cde.athabascau.ca/online_book/pdf/TPOL_chp15.pdf

Jorgensen, H. (2004). Illinois virtual campus-a cost effective, collaborative approach to online student support. *Distance Education Report, 8*(5), 8.

Lynch, M. V. (2001). Effective student preparation for online learning. *The Technology Source Archives, November/December.* Retrieved from http://technology-sourceorg/article/effective_student_preparation_for_online_learning/

Maddux, C. D. (2004). Developing online courses: Ten myths. *Rural Special Education Quarterly, 23*(2), 27–32.

Morgan, G. (2003). Key findings: Faculty use of course management systems. *Educause Center for Applied Research,* Retrieved from http://www.educause.edu/ir/library/pdf/ecar_so/ers/ers0302/ekf0302.pdf

Roblyer, M. D. (2006). Online high-school programs that work. *Education Digest, 72*(3), 55–63.

Roblyer, M. D., & Marshall, J. C. (2003). Predicting success of virtual high school students: Preliminary results from an educational success prediction instrument. *Journal of Research on Technology in Education, 35*(2), 241–255.

Santovec, M. L. (2005). Defining, supporting faculty excellence. *Distance Education Report, 9*(21), 1–2 and 6.

Scagnoli, N. I. (2001). Student orientations for online programs. *Journal of Research on Technology in Education, 34*(1), 19–27.

Smith, L., & Curry, M. (2005). Twelve tips for supporting online distance learners on medical post-registration courses. *Medical Teacher, 27*(5), 396–400.

Ullman, C., & Rabinowitz, M. (2004). Course management systems and the reinvention of instruction. *T.H.E. Journal, October,* 1–5. Retrieved from http://thejournal.com/articles/17014

Wheeler, S. (2006). Learner support needs in online problem-based learning. *The Quarterly Review of Distance Education,* 7(2), 175–184.

CHAPTER 3

THE LEARNER

This chapter will:

1. Identify the learner characteristics that should be considered in online course development, design, and implementation.
2. Identify and differentiate between cognitive styles.
3. Identify teaching and learning strategies to accommodate the cognitive styles.
4. Identify and differentiate between learning styles.
5. Identify teaching and learning strategies to accommodate the stages of learning.
6. Identify teaching and learning strategies to accommodate learning styles.
7. Identify and differentiate between the types of multiple intelligences.
8. Identify teaching and learning strategies to accommodate the types of multiple intelligences.

One of the first steps in online course development and design is to consider learner characteristics, cognitive styles, learning styles, and multiple intelligences. The educator should consider the learner throughout the

A Learner Centered Approach To Online Education, pages 29–45.

course development and design process. Teaching and learning strategies that accommodate a variety of cognitive styles, learning styles, and multiple intelligences should be incorporated into the course. This chapter includes information on the following topics: learner characteristics; cognitive styles; learning styles; and multiple intelligences.

LEARNER CHARACTERISTICS

Online course development, design, and implementation must consider the intended audience in order to facilitate and promote success (Minasian-Batmanian, 2002; Vrasidas & McIssac, 2002). There will be similarities and differences among the learners participating in the course or educational activity which can have an impact on the learning process and learning outcomes (Sheard & Lynch, 2003). Some learner characteristics to consider include: age, cultural background, educational background, occupational background, technical abilities, cognitive styles, learning styles, and multiple intelligences.

Age is an important learner characteristic that should be considered. Will there be a variety of ages participating? Will there be a specific age bracket? Course materials should be appropriate for the age of the audience. Undergraduate educators should consider that many high schools now allow students to participate in college courses for credit while enrolled in high school.

The cultural background of the learners is also an important characteristic to consider (Sheard & Lynch, 2003; Sutliff & Baldwin, 2001). The values and attitudes of the learner based on cultural background and family influences can have an impact on the learning process. Teaching and learning strategies should be designed to maximize learning outcomes.

The educational and occupational backgrounds are additional learner characteristics that should be considered (Edwards, 2005; Minasian-Batmanian, 2002; Sabry & Baldwin, 2003; Sheard & Lynch, 2003). Will the course be for K–12, undergraduate, or graduate level students? Will the course be for training or professional development? Do the learners have prior knowledge of the subject? Do the learners have occupational experience in regards to the subject matter (Sabry & Baldwin, 2003)? The course design and development will be impacted by the answers to these questions.

Next, the technological abilities of the learners should be considered (Minasian-Batmanian, 2002). Do the learners have experience with the technology that will be used? Will there be a required orientation course? Is this the learner's first online course? Educators may want to ask about online course experience at the beginning of the course. This will help identify students who may need additional help getting accustomed to the technology and the online learning experience.

COGNITIVE STYLES AND LEARNING STYLES

Other learner characteristics which are important to consider include cognitive styles (Sabry & Baldwin, 2003; Sheard & Lynch, 2003) and learning styles (Johnson & Aragon, 2003; Sheard & Lynch, 2003). In order to effectively *teach*, educators must understand the ways in which learners can *learn*. Learners have preferences in the way in which learning is approached and the learning strategies used, known as cognitive and learning styles respectively (Howard, 1995). Cognitive styles and learning styles can significantly impact the learning process and the learning outcomes (Cassidy, 2004; Sheard & Lynch, 2003; Xiaojing, Magjuka, & Lee, 2008). Some authors use the terms cognitive style and learning style interchangeably (Sheard & Lynch, 2003) while others define the terms somewhat differently. Sheard and Lynch (2003) described cognitive styles as "… a component or subset of learning styles" (p. 246).

Cognitive Styles

There are many definitions for cognitive styles available in the literature. A common component of the definitions available for cognitive styles is that cognitive styles are based on how a learner typically processes information (Cassidy, 2004; Cuthbert, 2005; DeTure, 2004; Howard, 1995; Merriam & Caffarella, 1999; Price, 2004; Xiaojing et al., 2008). Cognitive style "...involves attending, perceiving, remembering, and thinking" (Howard, 1995, p. 157) and is "...derived from cognitive controls and mental abilities" (Price, 2004, p. 683). There are a variety of models of cognitive styles available in the literature. A common model used for cognitive style incorporates the two dimensions of global-analytic and verbal-imagery.

Global-Analytic Dimension

The global-analytic dimension is based on how an individual organizes information (Riding & Grimley, 1999). Global learners organize information in wholes (Price, 2004; Riding & Grimley, 1999). Analytical learners organize information into parts (Price, 2004; Riding & Grimley, 1999).

Global learners see all concepts at once (Merriam & Caffarella, 1999). Global learners learn in a non-linear, random, holistic manner, and in large jumps (Sabry & Baldwin, 2003; Sheard & Lynch, 2003). Global learners learn best when they are able to see the big picture (Sabry & Baldwin, 2003; Sheard & Lynch, 2003) and when they are able to make connections between the information (Sabry & Baldwin, 2003). According to Howard (1995), "persons with a strong global style form overall impressions readily, are more intuitive, and mix feelings and facts" (p. 158). Global learners may benefit from presentations or learning activities that allow the learner to navigate through blocks of information in an unstructured manner.

Analytical learners prefer to learn in steps or stages (Merriam & Caffarella, 1999). Analytical learners learn in a linear (in small logical steps), organized, and detail oriented manner (Howard, 1995; Sabry & Baldwin, 2003). Analytical learners "...may not fully understand the material or establish a link with other parts, but are able to know a lot about specific aspects of the subject" (Sabry & Baldwin, 2003, p. 466). Analytical learners may benefit from presentations or learning activities that are structured with a step by step progression (Sabry & Baldwin, 2003).

Verbal-imagery Dimension

The verbal-imagery dimension is based on how an individual represents information during the thinking process (Riding & Grimley, 1999). This dimension is concerned with how learners process external stimuli (Price, 2004). Verbal learners use textual materials (Price, 2004) and represent information using verbal strategies (McKay, 1999; Riding & Grimley, 1999). Imagery learners use non-text materials (Price, 2004) and represent information using mental pictures (McKay, 1999; Riding & Grimley, 1999).

Learning Styles

There are many different ways learning styles can be defined and many surveys and assessments available for measuring learning styles. A common component of the definitions available for learning style is a preferred method or methods of learning (Cassidy, 2004; Howard, 1995; Klein, 2003; Price, 2004; Shearer, 2004). Learners may have a primary learning style (Denig, 2004). Learners may have more than one preferred learning style that could change over time and through learning experiences (Cassidy, 2004). Learners may also use a combination of learning styles (Denig, 2004; Silver, Strong, & Perini, 1997; Sutliff & Baldwin, 2001). Learners may have different learning styles based on the learning environment (Sheard & Lynch, 2003) and/or the learning task (Price, 2004).

It is important for educators to provide content in several formats and have a variety of teaching strategies to address all learning styles and individual differences among students (Ally, 2004; Burris, Kitchel, Molina, Vincent, & Warner, 2008; Chickering & Ehrmann, 1996; Denig, 2004; Douglas, Burton, & Reese–Durham; Guthbert, 2008; Johnson & Aragon, 2003; Koszalka & Ganesan, 2004; Mupinga, Nora, & Yaw, 2006; Sheard &Lynch, 2003; Sutliff & Baldwin, 2001). Learning outcomes are enhanced when learning styles are accommodated (Denig, 2004). Retention may also be increased when learning styles are accommodated (Sutliff & Baldwin, 2001).

There have been many models used to describe the methods, preferences, or styles learners use to approach the learning process. Two of the models will be explored. One model, the VAK Learning Styles Model, categorizes learning styles based on the sensory methods used in approaching the learning process. Another model, Kolb's Learning Styles, looks at learning as a four stage cycle from which four learning styles emerge.

VAK Learning Styles Model

The VAK Learning Styles Model includes three types of learning styles: visual, auditory, and kinesthetic/tactile. Visual learners learn best by seeing concepts and images. Auditory learners learn best by hearing concepts. Kinesthetic/tactile learners learn best by experiencing or doing.

The Visual Learner: There are a variety of learning and teaching strategies to accommodate the visual learner. The learner and educator can use pictures, charts, maps, diagrams, tables, spreadsheets, and flash cards to facilitate learning (Piedmont Education Services, 2006c; Three Rivers Community College, 2002c). Other learning and teaching strategies that can accommodate the visual learner include: collages, writing assignments, games, slide show presentations, puzzles (Piedmont Education Services, 2006c), and reading assignments. Visual learners also benefit from organizing materials (Three Rivers Community College, 2002c) and developing outlines. Videos and demonstrations are also helpful to the visual learner. Finally, visual learners should write down important information and highlight important concepts (Piedmont Education Services, 2006c; Three Rivers Community College, 2002c) to facilitate learning.

The Auditory Learner: There are a variety of learning and teaching strategies to accommodate the auditory learner. The learner and educator can use video with audio and recorded lectures to facilitate learning. Other learning and teaching strategies that can accommodate the auditory learner include: discussions, debates, oral presentations, reading flash cards out load, verbal games, demonstrations, and peer teaching (Piedmont Education Services, 2006a). Auditory learners also benefit from reading out loud while studying and being able to incorporate music, songs, and poems into their assignments (Piedmont Education Services, 2006a; Three Rivers Community College, 2002a).

The Kinesthetic/Tactile Learner: There are a variety of learning and teaching strategies to accommodate the kinesthetic/tactile learner. The educator should incorporate activities that require active participation (Piedmont Education Services, 2006b) to facilitate learning. Other learning and teaching strategies that can accommodate the kinesthetic/tactile learner include: note taking, dance, games, field trips, and role playing (Piedmont Education Services, 2006b; Three Rivers Community College, 2002b). Kinesthetic/tactile learners benefit from the use of return demonstrations and puzzles (Piedmont Education Services, 2006b). Kinesthetic/tactile learners would also benefit from the use of models and flashcards (Three Rivers Community College, 2002b).

Resource for VAK Learning Styles Model

The VAK Learning Style Quiz®	This web-site provides a self-assessment quiz from the Study and Learning Centre of RMIT University® to help identify one's preferred learning style of visual, auditory, or kinesthetic/tactile. http://www.dlsweb.rmit.edu.au/lsu/content/1_StudySkills/study_tuts/learning%20styles/vak.html

Kolb's Learning Styles

Kolb's Experiential Learning Model, developed by David A. Kolb in 1984, has four stages forming a cycle of learning (Cassidy, 2004; Kolb, 1998; Loo, 2004; Sutliff & Baldwin, 2001; Wang, Hinn, & Kanfer, 2001). The four stages of learning are: concrete experience, reflective observation, abstract conceptualization, and active experimentation (Cassidy, 2004; Kolb, 1998; Loo, 2004; Svinicki & Dixon, 1998). Kolb (1998) indicated that learners need to be able to move through all four stages. According to Svinicki and Dixon (1998), in order "… to produce a complete cycle, the instructor would select an activity from each pole and guide the students through them in order" (p. 579).

Concrete Experience: Concrete experience is the first stage of learning. During this stage of learning, students have some type of personal experience (Cassidy, 2004; Svinicki & Dixon, 1998) that promotes learning (Burris et al., 2008). "Students who prefer to learn through concrete experience value relationships with other people, make decisions based on intuition, and tend to be more concerned with feeling as opposed to thinking" (Burris et al., 2008, p. 45). Sutliff and Baldwin (2001) recommended personalized instruction during this stage of the learning cycle. Learning and teaching strategies useful during the concrete experience stage include: primary readings, video instruction, presentations, and demonstrations. Other learning and teaching strategies for this stage of learning include: laboratories, field work, simulations/games, problem sets, practical exercises, role playing, and small group discussion (Burris et al., 2008; Loo 2004; Sutliff & Baldwin, 2001; Svinicki & Dixon, 1998).

Reflective Observation: The second stage of learning is reflective observation. During this stage of learning, the learner observes (Loo, 2004), examines, and reflects on the learning experience (Cassidy, 2004; Svinicki & Dixon,

1998). During this stage, learners are able to consider many different points of view (Burris et al., 2008; Sutliff & Baldwin, 2001). Learning and teaching strategies useful during the reflective observation stage include: journaling, logs, discussions, reflective exercises, and observations. Brainstorming is also a useful learning and teaching strategy during this stage of learning (Burris et al., 2008; Loo, 2004; Svinicki & Dixon, 1998; Sutliff & Baldwin, 2001).

Abstract Conceptualization: The third stage in the learning cycle is abstract conceptualization. During this stage, the learner thinks, explains, and draws conclusions (Cassidy, 2004; Loo, 2004; Sivincki & Dixon, 1998). The learner uses logic and planning to approach a learning task (Burris et al., 2008; Sutliff & Baldwin, 2001). Learning and teaching strategies useful during the abstract conceptualization stage include: papers, projects, models, and critical thinking exercises. Analogies may also be a useful learning and teaching strategy during this stage (Burris et al., 2008; Svinicki & Dixon, 1998).

Active Experimentation: The final stage in the learning cycle is active experimentation. This stage of learning is characterized by application and doing (Cassidy, 2004; Loo, 2004; Svinicki & Dixon, 1998). During the active experimentation stage, learners look for practical solutions to a learning task (Sutliff & Baldwin, 2001). Learning and teaching strategies useful during the active experimentation stage include: hands on activities (Sutliff& Baldwin, 2001), case studies, fieldwork, projects, simulations, and return demonstration. Small group discussion may also be a useful learning and teaching strategy during this stage (Burris et al., 2008; Loo 2004; Svinicki & Dixon, 1998; Sutliff & Baldwin, 2001).

From the four stages of learning, Kolb proposed there are two independent dimensions of the model (Kolb, 1998; Wang et al., 2001). The first dimension is prehension (Cassidy, 2004) which is formed by concrete experimentation and abstract conceptualization (Kolb, 1998; Loo, 2004). Prehension "...represents the input of information either from experience or from abstractions" (Svinicki & Dixon, 1998, p. 578). Loo (2004) described prehension as the perceiving dimension.

The second dimension is transformation (Cassidy, 2004) which is formed by active experimentation and reflective observation (Kolb, 1998; Loo, 2004). Transformation "...refers to the processing of information by either internally reflecting on the experience or externally acting upon the conclusions which have been drawn" (Svinicki & Dixon 1998, p. 578). Loo (2004) described transformation as the processing dimension.

From these two dimensions, four types of learning styles emerge (Cassidy, 2004; Kolb, 1998; Loo, 2004; Wang et al., 2001). Each learning styles combines two of the four stages of learning. These learning styles are diverger, assimilator, converger, and accommodator.

Diverger: The diverger combines reflective observation with concrete experience (Cassidy, 2004; Kolb, 1998; Wang et al., 2001). The diverger looks at the learning situation from many view points (Loo, 2004; Sutliff & Baldwin, 2001; Wang et al., 2001). Divergers have an active imagination, are emotional (Kolb, 1998), and often find creative solutions (Cassidy, 2004). Refer to the learning and teaching strategies for the reflective observation and concrete experience stages discussed previously for strategies to accommodate the diverger.

Assimilator: The assimilator combines abstract conceptualization with reflective observation (Cassidy, 2004; Kolb, 1998; Sutliff & Baldwin, 2001; Wang et al., 2001). Assimilators are interested in abstract concepts and organize concepts in a logical manner (Loo, 2004; Wang et al., 2001). "They excel in inductive reasoning, in assimilating disparate observations into an integrated explanation" (Kolb, 1998 p. 131). Refer to the learning and teaching strategies for the abstract conceptualization and reflective observation stages discussed previously for strategies to accommodate the assimilator.

Converger: The converger combines abstract conceptualization with active experimentation (Cassidy, 2004; Sutliff & Baldwin, 2001; Wang et al., 2001). Convergers tend to do well on standardized tests with only one correct answer (Kolb, 1998) and finding practical applications for knowledge (Loo, 2004). Refer to the learning and teaching strategies for the abstract conceptualization and active experimentation stages discussed previously for strategies to accommodate the converger.

Accommodator: The accommodator combines active experimentation and concrete experience (Cassidy, 2004; Sutliff & Baldwin, 2001; Wang et al., 2001). Accommodators "...excel in situations that call for adaptation to specific immediate circumstances" (Kolb, 1998, p. 132). Accommodators prefer hands on learning (Cassidy, 2004; Loo, 2004; Wang et al., 2001) and trial and error (Kolb, 1998) in approaching a learning task. Refer to the learning and teaching strategies for the active experimentation and concrete experience stages discussed previously for strategies to accommodate the accommodator.

MULTIPLE INTELLIGENCES

Howard Gardner (2006) defined an intelligence as "... a computational capacity—a capacity to process a certain kind of information that originates in human biology and human psychology" (p. 6). Intelligence is characterized by the ability to solve problems and learn in certain ways. Initially, seven intelligences were identified by Gardner (Barrington, 2004; Denig, 2004; Douglas et al., 2008; Gardner, 2006; Hickey, 2004; McCoog, 2007; Noble, 2004; Shearer, 2004, Shepard, 2004). These intelligences included: verbal-linguistic, logical-mathematical, visual-spatial, kinesthetic, musical, interpersonal, intrapersonal. (Barrington, 2004; Denig, 2004; Burton, 2007; Douglas et al., 2008; Hickey, 2004; Lash, 2004; Matto, Berry–Edwards, Hutchison, Bryant, & Waldbillig, 2006; McCoog, 2007; Noble, 2004; Shepard, 2004). Gardner (2006), later identified naturalistic intelligence. One of the newest intelligences being considered by Gardner (2006) is existentialist intelligence. At the time of the publication of *Multiple Intelligences: New Horizons*, Gardner (2006) had not definitively named existentialist as the ninth intelligence. Individuals may have one or more dominant intelligences (Barrington, 2004; Gardner, 2006; Kezar, 2001). Each of the intelligences uses different methods of processing in the brain (Noble, 2004).

Verbal-Linguistic Intelligence

Verbal-linguistic intelligence is characterized by learning through the use of words and languages. Learners with dominate verbal-linguistic intelligence learn best using spoken and written languages (Amerson, 2006; Barrington, 2004; Denig, 2004; Douglas et al., 2008; Matto et al., 2006; Johnson & White, 2002; Nolen, 2003; Shearer, 2004; Shepard, 2004; Silver et al., 1997; Stanford, 2003). Learning is facilitated through audio, narration, writing, and reading.

There are a variety of learning and teaching strategies that accommodate the verbal-linguistic intelligence and facilitate learning. Some strategies include: reading assignments (Denig, 2004; Lash, 2004; Nolen, 2003); writing assignments, (Amerson, 2006; Denig, 2004; McCoog, 2007; Nolen, 2003), creative writing assignments (Lash, 2004; Shearer, 2004; Shepard, 2004); oral assignments (Denig, 2004; McCoog, 2007; Nolen, 2003), and storytelling (Amerson, 2006; Denig, 2004; Lash, 2004; Shearer, 2004; Shepard, 2004). Discussion, debate (Denig, 2004), and online chats (Nelson, 1998) are also useful strategies. Shearer (2004) recommended persuasive speeches to facilitate learning. Word games are another useful strategy (Amerson, 2006; Lash, 2004; Nelson, 1998) to facilitate learning. Finally, role play (Shepard, 2004), journal writing (Amerson, 2006), audio files, recorded lectures, and narrated slide show presentations are strategies to facilitate learning for learners with a dominant verbal-linguistic intelligence.

Logical-Mathematical Intelligence

Logical-mathematical intelligence is characterized by learning through the use of numbers. Learners with dominant logical-mathematical intelligence have the ability to manipulate numbers (Denig, 2004; Nolen, 2003;

Shearer, 2004; Silver et al., 1997). Learning is facilitated using abstract patterns, forming relationships (Barrington, 2004; Denig, 2004; Johnson &White, 2002; Kezar, 2001; Matto et al., 2006; Nolen, 2003; Prescott, 2001; Stanford, 2003), and solving problems.

There are a variety of learning and teaching strategies that accommodate the logical-mathematical intelligence and facilitate learning. Some strategies include: problem solving (Barrington, 2004; Denig, 2004; Lash, 2004; Matto et al., 2006; McCoog, 2007; Shepard, 2004; Shearer, 2004); mathematical operations (Matto et al., 2006; Shearer, 2004); number games (Amerson, 2006); projects using spread sheets or data bases (McCoog, 2007); and using manipulatives (Nolen, 2003). Brain teasers (Amerson, 2006); strategy games (Lash, 2004); categorization activities (Lash, 2004; Prescott, 2001); compare and contrast activities (Amerson, 2006: Shepard, 2004); explorations; and experiments (Prescott, 2001) are also useful strategies.

Visual- Spatial Intelligence

Visual-spatial intelligence is characterized by learning through the use of imagery and visualization (Amerson, 2006; Barrington, 2004; Denig, 2004; Nolen, 2003; Shearer, 2004; Shepard, 2004). Learners with dominant visual-spatial intelligence are able to visualize concepts in their mind. These learners also have a capacity to remember what they see.

There are a variety of learning and teaching strategies that accommodate visual-spatial intelligence and facilitate learning. Some strategies include: puzzles (Denig, 2004; Lash, 2004; Prescott, 2001); maze solving (Denig, 2004); using outlines (Amerson, 2006); charts (Prescott, 2001); and collages (Shepard, 2004). Maps (Prescott, 2001; Stanford, 2003), word games (Nelson, 1998), and drawing activities (Nolen, 2003) are also useful strategies. Other strategies include use of color pictures/photos (Amerson, 2006; Denig, 2004; Nolen, 2003) and other visuals (McCoog, 2007, Nolen, 2003; Shepard, 2004). Amerson (2006) recommended video clips and concept mapping. McCoog (2007) recommended creative assignments with video projects. Slide show presentations can also facilitate learning for learners with a dominant visual-spatial intelligence.

Kinesthetic Intelligence

Kinesthetic intelligence is characterized by the ability to use the body (Douglas et al., 2008; Kezar, 2001; Matto et al., 2006; Shearer, 2004; Silver et al., 1997; Stanford, 2003), touching (Denig, 2004; Lash 2004), and tools (Barrington, 2004; Denig, 2004; Silver et al., 1997) to process information in one's environment through bodily sensation (Amerson, 2006; Denig, 2004). Learners with a dominant kinesthetic intelligence need to have "hands on" participation in the learning process. These learners learn by doing.

There are a variety of learning and teaching strategies that accommodate kinesthetic intelligence and facilitate learning. Some strategies include: video production; virtual field trips (McCoog, 2007); return demonstration (Amerson, 2006); role play (Amerson, 2006; Prescott, 2001); and dance (Kezar, 2001; Shepard, 2004). Other strategies to facilitate learning for learners with dominant kinesthetic intelligence include: model building (Shepard, 2004; Sweet 1998); scavenger hunts (Shepard, 2004); and games involving movement (Kezar, 2001; Shepard, 2004).

Musical Intelligence

Musical intelligence is characterized by the capacity to use music, rhythm, pitch, tone, and timbre to learn (Amerson, 2006; Barrington, 2004; Denig, 2004; Douglas et al., 2008; Kezar, 2001; Lash, 2004; Matto et al., 2006; Nolen, 2003; Shearer, 2004; Shepard, 2004). Learners with dominant musical intelligence learn best using techniques such as singing (Amerson, 2006; Denig, 2004; Lash, 2004; Shearer, 2004; Silver et al., 1997). Learners with dominant musical intelligence can also learn by listening to music (Denig, 2004; Lash, 2004; Silver et al., 1997).

There are a variety of learning and teaching strategies that accommodate musical intelligence and promote learning. Some strategies include: interactive books; video; audio recordings; and projects that incorporate music (McCoog, 2007). Amerson (2006) recommended composing simple melodies for content mastery. Shepard (2004) recommended using songs that tell a story. Another strategy is to use music during assignments and activities (Amerson, 2006; Shepard, 2004) to facilitate learning for learners with a dominant musical intelligence. Finally, a recommended strategy is the use of games using music. Amerson (2006) supported this strategy and recommended musical chairs using content questions. Games using music can be created for the online environment.

Interpersonal Intelligence

Interpersonal intelligence is characterized by the ability to learn through the interaction with others (Amerson, 2006; Barrington, 2004; Douglas et al., 2008; Matto et al., 2006; McCoog, 2007; Shearer, 2004; Shepard, 2004; Stanford, 2003). Learners with dominant interpersonal intelligence are able to lead, organize others (Denig, 2004; Lash, 2004; Silver et al., 1997), and collaborate with others. Interpersonal intelligence is also characterized by the capacity to mentor and tutor others (Shepard, 2004).

There are several learning and teaching strategies that accommodate interpersonal intelligence and facilitate learning. Some strategies include presentations and video conferencing (McCoog, 2007). Other strategies include: interviews (Amerson, 2006; Denig, 2004); chats with individual students as facilitators; and word games (Nelson, 1998). Amerson (2006) also recommended strategies of networking and case studies with discussion. Group projects (Amerson, 2006; Nolen, 2003; Shepard, 2004; Stanford, 2003) and peer teaching assignments (Amerson, 2006; Lash, 2004; Shepard, 2004) are also effective strategies to facilitate learning for learners with a dominant interpersonal intelligence.

Intrapersonal Intelligence

Intrapersonal intelligence is characterized by self motivation (Barrington, 2004; Lash, 2004; McCoog, 2004), personal goal setting (Denig, 2004; Douglas et al., 2008; Lash, 2004; Shearer, 2004), and independence. Learners with a dominant intrapersonal intelligence are self directed. Learning is facilitated through self-assessment and reflection.

There are several learning and teaching strategies that accommodate intrapersonal intelligence and facilitate learning. Some strategies include: individual assignments (Amerson, 2006; Denig, 2004; Lash, 2004; Prescott, 2001); self-paced projects (Amerson, 2006; Denig, 2004; Prescott, 2001); reflection assignments (Amerson, 2006; Denig, 2004; Shepard, 2004; Stanford, 2003); and self-assessment activities (Shearer, 2004; Silver et al., 1997). McCoog (2007) recommended concept mapping, blogs, and internet research as effective strategies. Other strategies to facilitate learning for learners with dominant intrapersonal intelligence include journaling (McCoog, 2007; Shepard, 2004) and feedback with positive reinforcement (Nolen, 2003).

Naturalistic Intelligence

Naturalistic intelligence is characterized by the ability to make connections between content and the natural world (Barrington, 2004; Kezar, 2001; McCoog, 2007; Stanford, 2003). Learning is facilitated by classifying and categorizing information. Learning is also facilitated by working in nature (Amerson, 2006; Barrington, 2004; Denig, 2004; Douglas et al., 2008; Shearer, 2004); exploring living things (Amerson, 2006; Denig, 2004); and learning about plants and natural events (Amerson, 2006; Denig, 2004; Shepard 2004).

There are several learning and teaching strategies that accommodate naturalistic intelligence and facilitate learning. Some strategies include: videos, using data bases, and using spreadsheets (McCoog, 2007). Amerson (2006) recommended field trips to accommodate naturalistic intelligence. With advances in technology, field trips can be virtual or real. Other strategies to facilitate learning for learners with a dominant naturalistic intelligence include the use of nature photos (McCoog, 2007; Shepard, 2004) and outdoor class sessions or projects (Nolen, 2003).

Existentialist Intelligence

Existentialist intelligence is characterized by the ability to "… focus on the big picture and why the world operates the way it does" (McCoog, 2007, p. 27). Learners with dominant existentialist intelligence reflect on how their role fits into the big picture (Johnson & White, 2002). These learners also have "…the ability to engage large questions about existence" (Kezar, 2001, p. 143).

There are learning and teaching strategies that accommodate naturalistic intelligence and facilitate learning. One strategy is the use of collaborative web projects (McCoog, 2007). Other strategies to facilitate learning for learners with dominant existentialist intelligence include group discussions and reflection assignments.

CONCLUSION

One of the first steps in online course development and design is to consider the learner. The educator should consider the learner throughout the course development and design process. Teaching and learning strategies that accommodate a variety of cognitive styles, learning styles, and multiple intelligences should be incorporated into the online course or learning activity.

CHAPTER 3 APPLICATION EXERCISE

Identify a subject you teach or will teach and choose a module of instruction (examples: fractions, anatomy of the foot, specific history lesson, professionalism, wellness…) for that subject. It is recommended that you choose the first module that will be taught in your course.

Choose 2 *specific* teaching and/or learning activities for the module of instruction in your subject area that accommodates each of the areas addressed in this chapter. Complete the table below.

Subject:	Module of Instruction:
	Specific Teaching and/or Learning Activities (Specific to your content area and module of instruction)
Global Cognitive Style	
Analytic Cognitive Style	

Verbal Cognitive Style	
Imagery Cognitive Style	
Visual Learning Style	
Auditory Learning Style	
Kinesthetic Learning Style	
Concrete Experience Stage of Learning	
Reflective Observation Stage of Learning	
Abstract Conceptualization Stage of Learning	
Active Experimentation Stage of Learning	
Diverger Learning Style	
Assimilator Learning Style	
Converger Learning Style	
Accommodator Learning Style	
Verbal-Linguistic Intelligence	
Logical-Mathematical Intelligence	
Visual-Spatial Intelligence	
Kinesthetic Intelligence	
Musical Intelligence	
Interpersonal Intelligence	
Intrapersonal Intelligence	
Naturalistic Intelligence	
Existentialist Intelligence	

REFERENCES

Ally, M. (2004). Foundations of educational theory for online learning. In T. Anderson & F. Elloumi (Eds.), *Theory and practice of online learning* (pp. 3–31). Retrieved from http://cde.athabascauca/online_book/pdf/TPOL_chp01.pdf

Amerson, R. (2006). Energizing the nursing lecture: Application of the theory of multiple intelligence learning. *Nursing Education Perspectives, 27*(4), 194–196.

Barrington, E, (2004). Teaching to student diversity in higher education: How multiple intelligence theory can help. *Teaching in Higher Education, 9*(4), 421–434.

Burris, S., Kitchel, T., Molina, Q., Vincent, S., & Warner, W. (2008). The language of learning styles. *Techniques: Connecting Education and Careers, 83*(2), 44–48.

Burton, D. (2007). Psycho-pedagogy and personalized learning. *Journal of Education for Teaching, 33*(1), 5–17.

Cassidy, S. (2004). Learning styles: An overview of theories, models, and measures. *Educational Psychology, 24*(4), 419–444.

Chickering, A. W., & Ehrmann, S. C. (1996). Implementing the seven principles: Technology as a lever. *AAHE Bulletin, 49*(2), 3–6. Retrieved from http://aahea.org/bulletins/articles/sevenprinciples.htm.

Cuthbert, P. (2005). The student learning process: Learning styles or learning approaches. *Teaching in Higher Education, 10*(2), 235–249.

Denig, S. J. (2004). Multiple intelligences and learning styles: Two complimentary dimensions. *Teachers College Record, 106*(1), 96–111.

DeTure, M. (2004). Cognitive style and self-efficacy: Predicting student success in online distance education. *The American Journal of Distance Education, 18*(1), 21–38.

Douglas, O., Burton, K., & Reese–Durham, N. (2008). The effects of multiple intelligence teaching strategy on the academic achievement of eight grade math students. *Journal of Instructional Psychology, 35*(2), 182–187.

Edwards, P. (2005). Impact of technology on the content and nature of teaching and learning. *Nursing Education Perspectives, 26*(6), 344–347.

Gardner, H. (2006). *Multiple intelligences: New horizons.* New York, NY: Basic Books.

Hickey, M. G. (2004). Can I pick more than one project? Case studies of five teachers who used MI-based instructional planning. *Teachers College Record, 106*(1), 77–86.

Howard, R. (1995). *Learning and memory: Major ideas, principles, issues and applications.* Westport, CT: Praeger Publishers.

Johnson, K., & White, J. (2002). The use of multiple intelligences in criminal justice education. *Journal of Criminal Justice Education, 13*(2), 369–386.

Johnson, S. D., & Aragon, S. R. (2003). An instructional strategy framework for online learning environments. *New Directions for Adult and Continuing Education, 100,* 31–43.

Kezar, A. (2001). Theory of multiple intelligences: Implications for higher education. *Innovative Higher Education, 26*(2), 141–154.

Klein, P. D. (2003). Rethinking the multiplicity of cognitive resources and curricular representations: Alternatives to 'learning styles' and 'multiple intelligences'. *Journal of Curriculum Studies, 35*(1), 45–81.

Kolb, D. A. (1998). Learning styles and disciplinary differences. In K. A Feldman & M. B. Paulsen (Eds.), *Teaching and learning in the college classroom* (2nd ed.) (pp. 127–137). Boston, MA: Pearson Custom Publishing.

Koszalka, T. A., & Ganesan, R. (2004). Designing online courses: A taxonomy to guide strategic use of features available in course management systems (CMS) in distance education. *Distance Education, 25*(2), 243–256.

Lash, M. D. (2004). Multiple intelligences and the search for creative teaching. *Paths of Learning, 22,* 13–15.

Loo, R. (2004). Kolb's learning styles and learning preferences: Is there a linkage? *Educational Psychology, 24*(1), 99–108.

Matto, H., Berry–Edwards, J, Hutchison, E., Bryant, S., & Waldbillig, A. (2006). Teaching notes and exploratory study on multiple intelligences and social work education. *Journal of Social Work Education, 4*(2), 405–416.

McCoog, I. J. (2007). Integrated instruction: Multiple intelligences and technology. *The Clearing House, 81*(1), 25–28.

McKay, E. (1999). An investigation of text-based instructional materials enhanced with graphics. *Educational Psychology, 19*(3), 323–335.

Merriam, S., & Caffarella, R. (1999). *Learning in adulthood* (2nd ed.). San Francisco, CA: Jossey-Bass.

Minasian–Batmanian, L. C. (2002). Guidelines for developing an online learning strategy for your subject. *Medical Teacher, 24*(6), 645–657.

Mupinga, D. M., Nora, R. T., & Yaw, D. C. (2006). The learning styles, expectations, and needs of online students. *College Teaching, 54*(1), 185–189.

Nelson, G. (1998). Internet/web-based instruction and multiple intelligences. *Educational Media International, 35*(2), 90–94.

Noble, T. (2004). Integrating the revised Bloom's Taxonomy with multiple intelligences: A planning tool for curriculum differentiation. *Teachers College Record, 106*(1), 193–211.

Nolen, J. (2003). Multiple intelligences in the classroom. *Education, 124*(1), 115–119.

Piedmont Education Services (2006a). *Learning styles: Auditory.* Retrieved from http://www.pesdirect.com/lsiauditory.html.

Piedmont Education Services (2006b). *Learning styles: Tactile.* Retrieved from http://www.pesdirect.com/lsitactile.html.

Piedmont Education Services (2006c). *Learning styles: Visual.* Retrieved from http://www.pesdirect.com/lsivisual.html.

Prescott, H. M. (2001). Helping students say how they know what they know. *The Clearing House, 74*(6), 327–331.

Price, L. (2004). Individual differences in learning: Cognitive control, cognitive style, and learning style. *Educational Psychology, 24*(5), 681–698.

Riding, R., & Grimley, M. (1999). Cognitive style, gender, and learning from multimedia materials in 11-year-old children. *British Journal of Educational Technology, 30*(1), 43–56.

Sabry, K., & Baldwin, L. (2003). Web-based learning interaction and learning styles. *British Journal of Educational Technology, 34*(4), 443–454.

Sheard, J., & Lynch, J. (2003). Accommodating learner diversity in web-based learning environments: Imperatives for future developments. *International Journal of Computer Processing of Oriental Languages, 1*(4), 243–260.

Shearer, B. (2004). Multiple intelligence theory after 20 years. *Teachers College Record, 106*(1), 2–16.

Shepard, J. S. (2004). Multiple ways of knowing: Fostering resiliency through providing opportunities for participating in learning. *Reclaiming Children and Youth, 12*(4), 210–216.

Silver, H., Strong, S., & Perini, M. (1997). Integrating learning styles and multiple intelligences. *Educational Leadership, 55*(1), 22–27.

Sutliff, R., & Baldwin, V. (2001). Learning styles: Teaching technology subjects can be more effective. *The Journal of Technology Studies, 27*(1), 22–27. Retrieved from http://scholar.lib.vt.edu/ejournals/JOTS/Winter-Spring-2001/pdf/sutliff.pdf.

Svinicki, M. D., & Dixon, N. M. (1998). In K. A Feldman & M. B. Paulsen (Eds.), *Teaching and learning in the college classroom* (2nd ed.) (pp. 577–584). Boston, MA: Pearson Custom Publishing.

Sweet, S. (1998). A lesson learned about multiple intelligences. *Educational Leadership, 56*(3), 50–51.

Three Rivers Community College (2002a). *Auditory learning.* Retrieved from http://www.trcc.commnet.edu/ed_resources/tasc/Training/Auditory_Learning.htm.

Three Rivers Community College (2002b). *Tactile learning.* Retrieved from http://www.trcc.commnet.edu/ed_resources/tasc/Training/Tactile_Learning.htm.

Three Rivers Community College (2002c). *Visual learning.* Retrieved from http://www.trcc.commnet.edu/ed_resources/tasc/Training/Visual_Learning.htm.

Wang, X. C., Hinn, D. M., & Kanfer, A. G. (2001). Potential of computer supported collaborative learning for learners with different learning styles. *Journal of Research on Technology in Education, 34*(1), 75–85.

Vrasidas, C., & McIsaac, M. S. (2002). Principles of pedagogy and evaluation for web-based learning. *Educational Media International, 37*(2), 105–111.

Xiaojing, L., Magjuka, R., & Lee, S. (2008). The effects of cognitive styles, trust, conflict management, on online students' learning and virtual team performance. *British Journal of Educational Technology, 39*(5), 829–846.

CHAPTER 4

DOMAINS OF LEARNING

This chapter will:

1. Identify the uses of Bloom's Taxonomy.
2. Identify important concepts and teaching/learning strategies for each of the following domains: Cognitive, Affective, and Psychomotor.
3. Differentiate between the Dimensions and Categories of the Cognitive Domain.
4. Differentiate between the levels of the Affective Domain.
5. Differentiate between the levels of the Psychomotor Domain.

In order to write learning outcomes and instructional objectives, educators need to understand the Domains of Learning. In 1956, Dr. Benjamin Bloom led the development of Bloom's Taxonomy of Educational Objectives. The original Taxonomy has since been revised (Bumen, 2007; Chyung & Stepich, 2003; Krathwohl, 2002; Raths, 2002). Bloom's Taxonomy can assist educators in: developing learning objectives, choosing teaching strategies, preparing assessments, developing grading rubrics, and developing critical thinking skills for learners (Anderson et al., 2001; Bissell & Lemons, 2006; Bumen, 2007; Chyung & Stepich, 2003; Ganello, 2001; Krathwohl,

2002; Stenzel, 2006). The Taxonomy classifies learning into three domains: Cognitive (knowledge or thinking), Affective (attitudes or feelings), and Psychomotor (doing or motor skills).

THE COGNITIVE DOMAIN

The Cognitive Domain is concerned with knowledge acquisition, thinking, and intellectual outcomes (Gronlund & Brookhart, 2009). The revised taxonomy includes two dimensions within the Cognitive Domain: the Knowledge Dimension and the Cognitive Process Dimension (Anderson et al., 2001; Chyung & Stepich, 2003; Krathwohl, 2002). The Knowledge Dimension is concerned with the type of knowledge to be learned and has four progressive categories: Factual Knowledge, Conceptual Knowledge, Procedural Knowledge, and Metacognitive Knowledge (Anderson et al., 2001; Bumen, 2007; Krathwohl, 2002; Lam & McNaught, 2006). The Cognitive Process Dimension is concerned with those processes used to acquire knowledge and has six progressive categories: Remember, Understand, Apply, Analyze, Evaluate, and Create (Anderson et al., 2001).

The Knowledge Dimension

Factual Knowledge

Factual Knowledge includes basic fundamental facts associated with a discipline or subject (Anderson et al., 2001; Krathwohl, 2002). There are two categories of Factual Knowledge: Knowledge of Terminology and Knowledge of Specific Details and Elements (Anderson et al., 2001; Krathwohl, 2002). Knowledge of Terminology includes: basic vocabulary and terminology; labels; and symbols (Anderson et al., 2001). Knowledge of Specific Details and Elements includes "knowledge of events, locations, people, dates, sources of information, and the like" (Anderson et al., 2001, p. 47). Factual Knowledge is an important foundation for specific subject areas and disciplines. However, the higher levels of knowledge should be promoted and assessed for meaningful learning experiences (Mayer, 2002).

Conceptual Knowledge

There are three categories of Conceptual Knowledge including: Knowledge of Classifications and Categories; Knowledge of Principles and Generalizations; and Knowledge of Theories, Models, and Structures (Anderson et al., 2001; Krathwohl, 2002). Knowledge of Classification and Categories requires learners to be able to make connections and understand relationships between the basic fundamental facts associated with a discipline or subject (Anderson, 2001; Krathwohl, 2002). Knowledge of Principles and Generalizations requires that students know the "...particular abstractions that summarize observations of phenomena" (Anderson et al., 2001, p. 51).

Knowledge of Theories, Models, and Structures "…includes knowledge of the different paradigms, epistemologies, theories, and models that different disciplines use to describe, understand, explain, and predict phenomena" (Anderson et al., 2001. p. 52).

Procedural Knowledge

Procedural Knowledge is knowing a procedure (a sequence of steps to complete a task) or how to do something (Anderson et al., 2001). There are three categories of Procedural Knowledge: Knowledge of Subject-Specific Skills and Algorithms; Knowledge of Subject-Specific Techniques and Methods; and Knowledge of Criteria for Determining When to Use Appropriate Procedures. Knowledge of Subject-Specific Skills and Algorithms involves using a set of steps that result in a fixed end result (Anderson et al., 2001). Knowledge of Subject-Specific Techniques and Methods involves using techniques and methods that may not result in a fixed end result. Knowledge of Criteria for Determining When to Use Appropriate Procedures is knowledge of when to use specific procedures (Anderson et al., 2001).

Metacognitive Knowledge

There are three categories of Metacognitive Knowledge: Strategic Knowledge; Knowledge About Cognitive Tasks, Including Contextual and Conditional Knowledge; and Self Knowledge. Strategic Knowledge is the knowledge of learning strategies that can assist in learning in various content areas (Anderson et al., 2001; Raths, 2002). These strategies include: rehearsal strategies (repetition); elaboration strategies (mnemonics, paraphrasing, and summarizing); and organizational strategies (outlining, concept maps, and note taking) (Anderson et al., 2001). Elaboration strategies and organizational strategies are better at promoting comprehension than are rehearsal strategies (Anderson et al., 2001). Knowledge About Cognitive Tasks, Including Contextual and Conditional Knowledge is knowledge of when and why certain cognitive tasks are used (Anderson et al., 2001). Self Knowledge includes the ability to self-assess one's own strengths and weaknesses (Anderson et al., 2001).

The Cognitive Process Dimension

Remember

The Remember category of the Cognitive Process Dimension is used to promote retention (recognition or recall of information) and is an essential building block for the higher level cognitive processes (Anderson et al., 2001; Mayer, 2002). This level is characterized by memorization of information (Bissell & Lemons, 2006; Ganello, 2001; Penn State, 2007b). At this level, learners are able to recall and recognize information as it was presented to them, retrieving information from long term memory (Anderson et al., 2001; Chyung & Stepich, 2003; Ganello, 2001; Krathwohl, 2002).

Within the Remember category there are two cognitive processes: Recognizing and Recalling (Anderson et al., 2001). Recognizing is retrieving previously learned information from long term memory and determining if that information is consistent with newly presented material (Anderson et al., 2001). Recalling is retrieving information from long term memory when given clues or prompts (Anderson et al., 2001; Mayer, 2002).

Understand

The Understand category of the Cognitive Process Dimension, takes learning to a higher level than simply remembering information (Gronlund & Brookhart, 2009). At this level, the learner is able to grasp the meaning of oral, written, and graphic information (Anderson et al., 2001; Chyung & Stepich, 2003; Ganello, 2001; Gronlund & Brookhart, 2009) A basic level of understanding of information is demonstrated by the ability to: interpret, predict, and translate (Bissell & Lemons, 2006; Ganello, 2001; Gronlund & Brookhart, 2009; Penn State, 2007b). Understand is associated with transfer of learning (Anderson et al., 2001).

Within the Understand category, there are seven cognitive processes: Interpreting, Exemplifying, Classifying, Summarizing, Inferring, Comparing, and Explaining. Interpreting is converting information from one form to another (Anderson et al., 2001; Mayer, 2002) such as paraphrasing. Exemplifying is demonstrating understanding of a general concept or principle by giving specific examples or instances (Anderson et. al, 2001; Mayer, 2002). Classifying is determining that an example belongs to a certain category (Anderson et al, 2001; Mayer, 2002). Summarizing is the ability to produce a statement that represents important concepts, points, or themes from presented information (Anderson et al, 2001; Mayer, 2002). Inferring is the ability to make logical conclusions based on presented information (Mayer, 2002) and involves making comparisons (Anderson et al., 2001). Examples of inferring tasks include: analogies, completion tasks, and oddity tasks (Anderson et al., 2001). Comparing is the ability to identify similarities and differences between two or presented pieces of information or examples (Anderson et al, 2001; Mayer, 2002). Explaining is the ability to make information or concepts clear or understandable by developing and using a cause-and-effect model to determine how changes in individual components affect the other components (Anderson et al., 2001; Mayer, 2002).

Apply

Apply is the ability to take knowledge gained and apply that knowledge to new situations (Bissell & Lemons, 2006; Chyung & Stepich, 2003; Ganello, 2001; Gronlund & Brookhart, 2009; Krathwohl, 2002; Penn State, 2007b). Application requires a higher level of understanding than Remember and Understand (Gronlund & Brookhart, 2009). Apply is associated with transfer of learning (Anderson et al., 2001). Apply is linked with Procedural Knowledge (Knowledge Process Dimension) as it involves using procedures to perform exercise or solve problems (Anderson et. al., 2001; Mayer, 2002). Within the Apply category there are two cognitive processes: Executing and Implementing.

Executing is the ability to apply a procedure when presented with a familiar task (Anderson et al., 2001; Mayer, 2002). Skills and algorithms are associated with Executing (Anderson et al., 2001). Executing usually results in one correct answer (Anderson et al., 2001).

Implementing is the ability to apply a procedure when presented with an unfamiliar task (Anderson et al., 2001; Mayer, 2002). Implementing requires that students have an understanding of the possible procedures to solve the problem as well as the problem itself (Anderson et al, 2001). The use of techniques and methods is associated with Implementing and implementing may result in more than one answer (Anderson et al., 2001).

Analyze

Analyze is the ability to break down information into essential parts and determine the relationships between the parts and the whole (Anderson et al., 2001; Chyung & Stepich, 2003; Ganello, 2001; Gronlund & Brookhart, 2009; Krathwohl, 2002; Penn State, 2007b). Analyze is associated with transfer of learning (Anderson et al., 2001). Within the Analyze category, there are three cognitive processes: Differentiating, Organizing, and Attributing. Differentiating is the ability to discriminate relevant or important from irrelevant or unimportant information (Anderson et al., 2001; Mayer, 2002). Organizing is the ability to structure presented material in some manner such as an outline or table (Anderson et al., 2001; Mayer, 2002). Attributing is the ability to determine biases, values, intent, or point of view of presented information (Anderson et al., 2001, Mayer, 2002).

Evaluate

Evaluate is the ability to make judgments based on clearly defined criteria and standards (Anderson et al., 2001; Chyung & Stepich, 2003; Gronlund & Brookhart, 2009; Mayer, 2002; Stepich, 2003; Krathwohl, 2002; Penn State, 2007b). Evaluate is associated with transfer of learning (Anderson et al., 2001). Within the Evaluate category there are two cognitive processes: Checking and Critiquing. Checking involves making judgments about internal consistency of information (Anderson et al., 2001; Mayer, 2002). Critiquing involves making judgments based on external criteria (Anderson et al., 2001; Mayer, 2002). Judgments are based on positive and negative attributes and other stated criteria (Anderson et al, 2001). The ability to critique is essential for critical thinking (Anderson et al., 2001; Mayer, 2002).

Create

Create is the ability to pull parts together to form or produce an original product (Anderson et al., 2001; Chyung & Stepich, 2003; Ganello, 2001; Gronlund & Brookhart, 2009; Krathwohl, 2002; Mayer, 2002). Create is associated with transfer of learning (Anderson et al., 2001). Within the Create category, there are three cognitive processes: Generating, Planning, and Producing. Generating is attempting to understand a given task and generate possible solutions to the task (Anderson et al., 2001; Mayer, 2002). Planning is deciding on a solution and developing an action plan (Anderson et al., 2001; Mayer, 2002). Producing is implementing the action plan into an original product or solution (Anderson et al., 2001; Mayer, 2002).

THE AFFECTIVE DOMAIN

The Affective Domain is concerned with attitudes, feelings, and values. (Gronlund & Brookhart, 2009). The Affective Domain is an important part of learning in the following subjects or content areas: sales techniques, patient interactions, employee management, ethics, team work, innovation, leadership, conflict management, motivation (Adkins, 2004), and professionalism. The Affective Domain allows the learner to put the content into the context of their own lives and careers (Bolin, Khramtsova, & Saarnio, 2005). Instruction that emphasizes learning in the Affective Domain can promote learning, student satisfaction, and retention. (Bolin et al., 2005).

There are five progressive levels within the Affective Domain. These five levels include: Receiving, Responding, Valuing, Organizing, and Characterization (Gronlund & Brookhart, 2009; Penn State, 2007a; Stenzel, 2006). Receiving occurs when the student is aware of (attending) a learning task or activity and is willing to listen and receive the information (Gronlund & Brookhart, 2009; Penn State, 2007a; Stenzel, 2006). Responding occurs when the student is an active participant in the learning task or activity (Gronlund & Brookhart, 2009; Stenzel, 2006). "Learning outcomes in this area may emphasize acquiescence in responding (reads assigned material), willingness to respond (voluntarily reads beyond the assignment), or satisfaction in responding (reads for pleasure or enjoyment)" (Gronlund & Brookhart, 2009, p. 130). Valuing occurs when the student attaches worth or value to the information being learned (Stenzel, 2006) and is associated with attitudes and appreciation (Gronlund & Brookhart, 2009). Organizing occurs when the student integrates the new values being learned into his/her value system (Gronlund & Brookhart, 2009; Penn State, 2007a; Stenzel,

2006). Characterization occurs when the new value has a consistent impact on behavior (Penn State, 2007a; Stenzel, 2006).

THE PSYCHOMOTOR DOMAIN

The Psychomotor Domain is concerned with motor skills and doing. One classification system for the Psychomotor Domain has seven progressive levels. These levels include: Perception, Set, Guided Responses, Mechanism, Complex Overt Response, Adaptation, and Origination. In the Perception category, physical or motor activity is guided through sensory cues (Gronlund & Brookhart, 2009; Huitt, 2003). The Set category includes the mental, physical, and emotional readiness to perform a certain physical or motor task (Gronlund & Brookhart, 2009; Huitt, 2003). In the Guided Responses category, learners begin to learn a physical or motor skill through imitation and practice (Gronlund & Brookhart, 2009; Huitt, 2003). In the Mechanism category, learners are able to perform a physical or motor skill at an intermediate level of proficiency (Gronlund & Brookhart, 2009; Huitt, 2003). In the Complex Overt Response category, learners are able to perform highly coordinated physical or motor skills at an advanced level of proficiency (Gronlund & Brookhart, 2009; Huitt, 2003). In the Adaptation category, learners are able to adapt and modify physical and motor skills depending on the situation (Gronlund & Brookhart, 2009; Huitt, 2003). In the Origination category, learners are able to develop a new physical or motor skill derived from skills previously learned (Gronlund & Brookhart, 2009; Huitt, 2003).

CONCLUSION

Bloom's Taxonomy can assist educators in: developing learning objectives, choosing teaching strategies, preparing assessments, developing grading rubrics, and developing critical thinking skills for learners (Anderson et al., 2001; Bissell & Lemons, 2006; Bumen, 2007; Chyung & Stepich, 2003; Ganello, 2001; Krathwohl, 2002; Stenzel, 2006). With an understanding of the Domains of Learning, learning outcomes and instructional objectives can be written. Educators should include instructional objectives that promote higher levels of learning within the Domains, not just remembering and understanding.

CHAPTER 4 APPLICATION EXERCISE

Use the same subject and module of instruction that you used for the Application Exercises for Chapter 3. Identify two learning/teaching strategies appropriate for each level of the Cognitive Domain (Remember, Understand, Apply, Analyze, Evaluate, and Create). Complete the table below.

	Specific Strategies (Specific to your content area and module of instruction)
Remember	
Understand	
Apply	
Analyze	
Evaluate	
Create	

REFERENCES

Adkins, S. (2004). Beneath the tip of the iceberg. *Training and Development, 58*(2), 28–33.

Anderson, L. W., Krathwohl, D. R., Airasian, P. W., Cruikshank, K. A., Mayer, R. E., Pintrich, P. R., Raths, J., & Wittrock, M. C. (2001). *A taxonomy for learning, teaching, and assessing* (Abridged ed.). New York, NY: Addison Wesley Longman, Inc.

Bissell, A. N., & Lemons, P. P. (2006). A new method for assessing critical thinking in the classroom. *BioScience, 56*(1), 66–72.

Bolin, A., Khramtsova, I., & Saarnio, D. (2005). Using student journals to stimulate authentic learning: Balancing Bloom's cognitive and affective domains. *Teaching of Psychology, 32*(3), 154–159.

Bumen, N. T. (2007). Effects of the original versus revised Bloom's taxonomy on lesson planning skills: A Turkish study among pre-service teachers. *Review of Education, 53*, 439–455.

Chyung, S., & Stepich, D. (2003). Applying the "congruence" principle of Bloom's taxonomy to designing of online instruction. *The Quarterly Review of Distance Education, 4*(3), 317–330.

Ganello, D. H. (2001). Promoting cognitive complexity in graduate written work: Using Bloom's taxonomy as a pedagogical tool to improve literature reviews. *Counselor Education and Supervision, 40*, 292–307.

Gronlund, N. E., & Brookhart, S. M. (2009). *Gronlund's writing instructional objectives* (8th ed). Upper Saddle River, NJ: Pearson Education, Inc.

Huitt, W. (2003). The psychomotor domain. In *Educational Psychology Interactive*. Valdosta, GA: Valdosta State University. Retrieved from http://chiron.valdosta.edu/whuitt/col/behsys/psymtr.html

Krathwohl, D. R. (2002). A revision of Bloom's taxonomy: An overview. *Theory Into Practice, 41*(4), 212–218.

Lam, P., & McNaught, C. (2006). Design and evaluation of online courses containing media-enhanced learning materials. *Educational Media International, 43*(3), 199–218.

Mayer, R. W. (2002). Rote versus meaningful learning. *Theory Into Practice, 41*(4), 226–232.

Penn State. (2007a). Affective domain taxonomy. In *Teaching and learning with technology*. Retrieved from http://www.tlt.psu.edu/suggestions/research/Affective_Taxonomy.shtml

Penn State. (2007b). Bloom's taxonomy of cognitive objectives. In *Teaching and learning with technology*. Retrieved from http://www.tlt.psu.edu/suggestions/research/Blooms_Taxonomy.shtml

Raths, J. (2002). Improving instruction. *Theory Into Practice, 41*(4), 233–237.

Stenzel, E. J. (2006). A rubric for assessing in the affective domain for retention purposes. *Assessment Update, 18*(3), 9–11.

CHAPTER 5

LEARNING OUTCOMES AND INSTRUCTIONAL OBJECTIVES

This chapter will:

1. Distinguish between learning outcomes and instructional objectives.
2. Identify the components of instructional objectives.

This chapter includes information on writing instructional objectives. Information will be provided on the audience and behavior (verbs for the cognitive domain, verbs for the affective domain; and verbs for the psychomotor domain) components of instructional objectives. Information will also be provided on the condition and degree components of instructional objectives.

BACKGROUND INFORMATION

Many academic programs have established the overall program learning outcomes and the learning outcomes for individual courses. Accrediting associations and other governing bodies may require specific learning out-

A Learner Centered Approach To Online Education, pages 57–65.
Copyright © 2013 by Information Age Publishing

comes for programs. Learning outcomes are broadly stated and focus on the program or course as a whole (Anderson et al., 2001; Caffarella, 2002). A learning outcome should be broken down into the individual steps or components the learner will need to be able to do to meet the learning outcome. These steps or components become the foundation for the instructional objectives which assist the educator in planning units or modules of instruction within a course (Anderson et al., 2001). Instructional objectives should reflect specifically and objectively what the learner should be able to do as a result of the instruction (Gronlund & Brookhart, 2009; Mager, 1997).

Here is an example:

Learning Outcome: Write instructional objectives.

Instructional Objectives

1. Upon completion of this module of instruction, the learner will be able to define each component of the ABCD formula for writing instructional objectives, as determined by a score of 100% on the corresponding assignments and assessments.

2. Upon completion of this module of instruction, the learner will be able to determine the ABCD of instructional objectives, as determined by a score of 100% on the corresponding assignments and assessments.

3. Upon completion of this module of instruction, the learner will be able to identify verbs describing what the learner should be able to do for each of the categories in the Cognitive Process Dimension, the Affective Domain, and the Psychomotor Domain, as determined by a score of 80% on the corresponding assignments and assessments.

4. Upon completion of this module of instruction, the learner will be able to identify properly written objectives addressing the Cognitive Domain, applying the ABCD format, as determined by a score of 80% on the corresponding assignments and assessments.

5. Upon completion of this module of instruction, the learner will be able to identify properly written objectives addressing the Psychomotor Domain, applying the ABCD format, as determined by a score of 80% on the corresponding assignments and assessments.

6. Upon completion of this module of instruction, the learner will be able to identify properly written objectives addressing the Affective Domain, applying the ABCD format, as determined by a score of 80% on the corresponding assignments and assessments.

7.   Upon completion of this module of instruction, the learner will successfully create a minimum of four instructional objectives derived from one learning outcome in his/her content area addressing at least four levels of the Cognitive Process Dimension (using ABCD format) as determined by a score of 80% on the corresponding assignments and assessments.

A complete list of instructional objectives needed to achieve the overall learning outcome would be written. In the case of the example learning outcome, there are seven instructional objectives.

WRITING INSTRUCTIONAL OBJECTIVES

Writing good instructional objectives takes practice and improves over time. A common formula for writing instructional objectives is the ABCD formula: The A is the audience. The B is the behavior. The C is the condition(s). The D is the degree.

Audience

The audience can be specified as a student, a learner, a participant, a trainee, a patient, etc. The audience is NOT the educator. The audience may be assumed and is not always included in the written objective. For the purposes of this chapter, the audience will be included in the instructional objective.

In the following learning objective example, the audience is "the student".

Upon completion of this module of instruction, *the student* will be able to successfully write objectives addressing the Cognitive Domain, applying the ABCD format, as determined by a score of 80% on the corresponding assignment.

Behavior

The behavior is what the learner should be able to do as a result of the instruction. The behavior usually includes a verb describing the process and a noun describing the knowledge, area of content, or type of skill (Anderson et al., 2001). In the cognitive domain, the verb reflects the cognitive process dimension and the noun reflects the knowledge dimension (Anderson et al., 2001).

In the following learning objective example from the Cognitive Domain, the behavior is "label the states".

Given a blank map of the United States, the student will be able to successfully *label the states* as noted by a score of 80% on the corresponding test.

Label is the verb. This is a verb used to describe what a student should be able to do at the remember level of the Cognitive Process Dimension of the Cognitive Domain.

States is the noun. This noun represents the Factual Knowledge level of the Knowledge Process Dimension of the Cognitive Domain

Behavior: Verbs for the Cognitive Domain

Cognitive Process Category	Verbs to describe what the learner should be able to…
Remember (includes Recognizing and Recalling)	cite, count, circle, define, draw, describe, explain, identify, label, list, match, name, outline, recall, recognize, record, relate, repeat, reproduce, retrieve, select, state, tell, underline, write (Gronlund & Brookhart, 2009; Huitt, 2004; Penn State, 2007)
Understand (includes Interpreting, Exemplifying, Classifying, Summarizing, Inferring, Comparing, and Explaining)	categorize, choose, cite examples of, classify, clarify, compare, conclude, contrast, convert, defend, distinguish, demonstrate use of, describe, determine, differentiate between, discriminate, discuss, estimate, exemplify, explain, express, extend, extrapolate. generalize, give in own words, identify, illustrate, infer, interpret, locate, map, match, paraphrase, pick, practice, predict, recognize, select, represent, report, respond, restate, review, rewrite, simulate, summarize, tell, translate (Anderson et al., 2001; Gronlund & Brookhart, 2009; Huitt, 2004; Krathwohl, 2002; Mayer, 2002; Penn State, 2007)
Apply (includes Executing and Implementing)	apply, carry out, change, compute, construct, discover, dramatize, employ, generalize, illustrate, initialize, initiate, interpret, manipulate, modify, operate, operationalize, practice, predict, prepare, produce relate, schedule, shop, show, solve, use (Gronlund & Brookhart, 2009; Huitt, 2004; Penn State, 2007)

Analyze (includes Differentiating, Organizing, and Attributing)	analyze, appraise, break down; calculate, categorize, compare, conclude, contrast, correlate, criticize, deconstruct, deduce, debate, detect, determine, develop, diagram, differentiate, discriminate, distinguish, draw conclusions, estimate, evaluate, examine, experiment, identify, illustrate, infer, inspect, integrate, inventory, outline, predict, points out, question, relate, selects, separate, solve, test, diagnose (Gronlund & Brookhart, 2009; Huitt, 2004; Penn State, 2007)
Evaluate (includes Checking and Critiquing)	appraise, assess, choose, compare, conclude, contrast, critique, describe, detect, discriminate, estimate, explain, evaluate, judge, justify, interpret, measure, rate, recommend, relate, revise, score, select, summarize, support, validate, value, test (Gronlund & Brookhart, 2009; Huitt, 2004; Penn State, 2007)
Create (includes Generating, Planning, and Producing)	arrange, assemble, categorize, collect, combine, compiles, compose, construct, create, design, develop, devise, explain, formulate, generate, hypothesize, invent, manage, modify, organize, plan, prepare, produce, propose, predict, rearrange, reconstruct, relate. revise, set-up, synthesize, systematize, write (Gronlund & Brookhart, 2009; Huitt, 2004; Penn State, 2007)

Behavior: Verbs for the Affective Domain

Category	Verbs to describe what the learner should be able to…
Receiving	accept, attend, ask, choose, describe, develop, follow, give, hold, identify, locate, name, point to, realize, receive, recognize, reply, selects, sits erect, uses (Coastal Carolina University, 2009; Gronlund & Brookhart, 2009; Shepard & Jensen, 2002)

Responding	behave, aide, answer, assist, complete, comply, conform, cooperate, discuss, examine, greet, help, label, perform, practice, present, obey, observe, reads, recites, reports, respond, selects, tells, writes (Coastal Carolina University, 2009; Gronlund & Brookhart, 2009; Shepard & Jensen, 2002)
Valuing	accept, balance, believe, complete, defend, describe, devote, differentiate, explain, follow, form, influence, initiate, invite, join, justify, prefer, propose, pursue, read, report, seek, select, share, study, value, work (Coastal Carolina University, 2009; Gronlund & Brookhart, 2009; Shepard & Jensen, 2002)
Organizing	adhere, alter, arrange, combine, compare, complete, defend, discriminate, display, explain, favor, judge, generalize, identify, integrate, modify, order, organize, prepare, relate, synthesize, weigh (Coastal Carolina University, 2009; Gronlund & Brookhart, 2009; Shepard & Jensen, 2002)
Characterization	act, demonstrate, discriminate, display, influence, listen, modify, perform, practice, propose, qualify, question, revise, serve, solve, use, value (Coastal Carolina University, 2009; Gronlund & Brookhart, 2009)

Behavior: Verbs for the Psychomotor Domain

Category	Verbs to describe what the learner should be able to...
Perception	choose, describe, detect, differentiate, distinguish, hear, identify, isolate, relate, see, select, separate, smell, taste, touch (Gronlund & Brookhart, 2009; Huitt, 2003; Shepard & Jensen, 2002)

Set	adjust, approach, assume a position, begin, demonstrate, display, explain, locate, move, place, position, prepare, proceed, react, respond, show, start, volunteer Gronlund & Brookhart, 2009; Huitt, 2003; Shepard & Jensen, 2002)
Guided Responses	assemble, attempt, build, calibrate, construct, copy, determine, discover, dismantle, display, dissect, duplicate, fasten, fix, grind, heat, imitate, inject, manipulate, measure, mend, mix, organize, repeat, try (Gronlund & Brookhart, 2009; Huitt, 2003; Shepard & Jensen, 2002)
Mechanism	adjust, assemble, build, calibrate, construct, dismantle, display, dissect, fasten, fix, grind, heat, illustrate, indicate, manipulate, measure, mend, mix, organize, set up, sketch, works (Gronlund & Brookhart, 2009; Shepard & Jensen, 2002)
Complex Overt Response	assemble, build, calibrate, carry out, construct, coordinate, demonstrate, dismantle, display, dissect, fasten, fix, grind, heat, manipulate, maintain, measure, mend, mix, operate, organize, perform, sketch, work (Gronlund & Brookhart, 2009; Huitt, 2003; Shepard & Jensen, 2002)
Adaptation	adapt, alter, build, change, develop, modify, rearrange, reorganize, revise, supply (Gronlund & Brookhart, 2009; Huitt, 2003; Shepard & Jensen, 2002)
Origination	arrange, combine, compose, construct, create, design, produce, originate (Gronlund & Brookhart, 2009; Huitt, 2003; Shepard & Jensen, 2002)

Condition

The condition is the how or when of the objective. The condition includes any special circumstances (Mager, 1997). In the following learning objective example, the condition is "Upon completion of this module of instruction".

Upon completion of this module of instruction, the student will be able to successfully write objectives addressing the Cognitive Domain, applying the ABCD format, as determined by a score of 80% on the corresponding assignment.

Degree

The degree is the acceptable level of performance or competence (Mager, 1997). In the following learning objective example, the degree is "a score of 80% on the corresponding assignment".

Upon completion of this module of instruction, the student will be able to successfully write objectives addressing the Cognitive Domain, applying the ABCD format, as determined by a score of 80% on the corresponding assignment.

CONCLUSION

Educators should include instructional objectives based on the Domains of Learning that promote higher levels of learning, not just remembering and understanding. Instructional objectives provide the foundation for decisions about instruction. Instructional objectives are also important in course evaluation (Gronlund & Brookhart, 2009; Mager, 1997). Once the specific instructional objectives have been written; learning, teaching, and assessment strategies that align with the instructional objectives can be chosen for each unit or module of instruction in the course.

CHAPTER 5 APPLICATION EXERCISE

Use the same subject and module of instruction that you used for the Application Exercises for Chapter 3 and Chapter 4. Write one learning outcome for the module of instruction. Write four instructional objectives for the learning outcome addressing at least four levels of the Cognitive Process Dimension.

Learning Outcome:

Instructional Objective 1

Instructional Objective 2

Instructional Objective 3

Instructional Objective 4

REFERENCES

Anderson, L. W., Krathwohl, D. R., Airasian, P. W., Cruikshank, K. A., Mayer, R. E., Pintrich, P. R., Raths, J., & Wittrock, M. C. (2001). *A taxonomy for learning, teaching, and assessing* (Abridged ed.). New York; Addison Wesley Longman, Inc.

Caffarella, R. (2002). *Planning programs for adult learners.* San Francisco, CA: Jossey-Bass

Coastal Carolina University (2009). *Bloom's taxonomy.* Retrieved from www.coastal. edu/cetl/IDP%20presentation%20materials/three%20domains.pdf

Gronlund, N. E., & Brookhart, S. M. (2009). *Gronlund's writing instructional objectives* (8th ed.). Upper Saddle River, NJ: Pearson Education, Inc.

Huitt, W. (2003). The psychomotor domain. *Educational Psychology Interactive.* Valdosta, GA: Valdosta State University. Retrieved from http://www.edpsycinteractive.org/topics/behavior/psymtr.html

Huitt, W. (2004). Bloom et al.'s taxonomy of the cognitive domain. *Educational Psychology Interactive.* Valdosta, GA: Valdosta State University. Retrieved from http://chiron.aldostadu/whuitt/col/cogsys/bloom.html

Krathwohl, D. R. (2002). A revision of Bloom's taxonomy: An overview. *Theory Into Practice, 41*(4), 212–218.

Mager, R. F. (1997). *Preparing instructional objectives* (3rd ed.). Atlanta, Georgia: CEP Press.

Mayer, R. W. (2002). Rote versus meaningful learning. *Theory Into Practice, 41*(4), 226–232.

Penn State. (2007). Bloom's taxonomy of cognitive objectives. In *Teaching and learning with technology.* Retrieved from http://www.tlt.psu.edu/suggestions/research/Blooms_Taxonomy.shtml

Shepard, G., & Jensen, G. M. (2002). *Handbook of teaching for physical therapists.* Woburn, MA: Butterworth-Heinemann.

CHAPTER 6

ONLINE COURSE INTERACTION

This chapter will:

1. Identify the factors to be considered when delivering course content and choosing learning and teaching strategies for the online course.
2. Identify methods of student-content interaction and the resources to incorporate student-content interaction into the online course.
3. Identify the uses, advantages, and disadvantages for specific student-content methods/strategies.
4. Identify methods of student-student interaction and the resources to incorporate student-student interaction into the online course.
5. Identify the advantages, disadvantages, and strategies for incorporating specific student-student methods/strategies in an online course.
6. Identify methods of student-educator interaction that should be incorporated into the online course.
7. Identify characteristics of effective feedback.

After the learning outcomes and instructional objectives have been developed, the educator should choose methods of content delivery, learning

A Learner Centered Approach To Online Education, pages 67–116.

strategies, teaching strategies, and other resources that allow and facilitate interaction (Cuellar, 2002; Northrup, 2002). Northrup (2002) defined interaction as "...engagement in learning" (p. 219). There are three types of interaction that should occur in an online course: student-content, student-student, and student-educator (Ascough, 2002; Barbera, 2004; Berge, 2002; Hirumi, 2002; Northrup 2002; Wanstreet, 2006; Yoon, 2003). Online course developers, designers, and educators should strive to make the online course engaging for all learners. Northrup (2002) indicated that interaction promotes learner satisfaction and facilitates student retention. The educator should consider the characteristics, cognitive styles, learning styles, and multiple intelligences of the learner when selecting methods of content delivery, learning strategies, teaching strategies, and other resources for an online course. The educator should also consider the instructional objectives, corresponding level(s) of knowledge, and domains of learning when selecting methods of content delivery, learning strategies, teaching strategies, and other resources for an online course.

PART I: STUDENT-CONTENT INTERACTION

The first part of this chapter includes information on the following topics: text-based documents; Microsoft Office Power Point® presentation software and Microsoft Office Power Point® presentation software add ins/ plug ins; graphics, images, and photos; audio, video; screen capture and screen recording; and podcasting. Information on case-based instruction; animation; simulation and virtual reality; games; learning objects and online lessons; web quests; papers and projects; portfolios; and journals is also included. Finally, online resources; online resources by discipline; and additional instructional resources are provided.

The online course should be broken down into modules or units of instruction. For each module or unit of instruction, content and learning materials should be selected and sequenced appropriately (Ally, 2004; Carr–Chellman & Duchastel, 2001; Koszalka & Ganesan, 2004; Sims, Dobb, & Hand, 2002). The online content and learning materials should be "chunked" into small blocks or lessons to facilitate learning and prevent information overload (Ally, 2004; Carr–Chellman & Duchastel, 2001; Johnson & Aragon, 2003; Ruiz, Mintze, & Issenberg, 2006; Shi, Bonk, & Magjuka, 2006).

Student-content interaction is about providing opportunities for the learner to have active participation and interaction in the learning process (Ally, 2004; Anderson, 2004; Buckley & Smith, 2007; Caplan, 2004; Chickering & Ehrmann, 1996; Johnson & Aragon, 2003; Koszalka & Ganesan, 2004; Norton & Hathway, 2008; Sims et al., 2002), not just about presenting content. Interaction with the content provides opportunities for the learner to process and organize the content and materials (Berge, 2002; Hirumi, 2002) as well as apply concepts (Berge, 2002). Opportunities for interaction with the content should accommodate different learning styles (Yoon, 2003), provide opportunities for practice (Sieber, 2005), provide self-assessment activi-ties (Ally, 2004; Anderson, 2004; Hirumi, 2002; Sieber, 2005), and provide op-portunities for reflection (Berge, 2002; Sieber, 2005). Links to supplemental resources should also be provided (Koszalka & Ganesan, 2004).

A multi-media approach should be used when developing and delivering an online course in order to facilitate student-content interaction (Koszalka & Ganesan, 2004). Multimedia can be defined as "presenting information through multiple processes including but not limited to text, audio, graph-ics, animation, and video" (Buckley & Smith, 2007, p. 58). Multimedia can be used to enhance the content from text books or other sources (Buckley & Smith, 2007) and should directly relate to instruction (Hawkes & Coldeway, 2002).

The educator should seek available resources from the institution, text book publishers, and/or other outside resources. The educator's institution may have developed or purchased resources that can be used for courses. Within the institution, other educators may also be willing to share resources. Some text book publishers provide presentations, interactive activities, quiz ques-tions, discussion questions, and other resources and materials to supplement text books. Some text book publishers also provide course cartridges that can be downloaded into the course management system. Outside resources in-clude: web-sites, commercial products, free products, learning object reposito-ries, etc. If appropriate resources are not available, the educator should create the resources which will require access to the necessary software.

Text-Based Documents

Text-based documents can be basic word processing documents, web pages, and portable document format (PDF) files. Some of these file types/ resources may provide capabilities for interaction and others do not. Text-based documents should not be the primary means of content delivery.

Resources for Text-Based Documents

Microsoft Office Word®	This is a commercial word processing software by Microsoft®. http://office.microsoft.com/en-us/word/FX100487981033.aspx
Microsoft Office Word Viewer®	Learners will need the free Microsoft Office Word Viewer® if Microsoft Office Word® is not already installed on their computer. turhttp://www.microsoft.com/downloads/details.aspx?FamilyID=3657ce88-7cfa-457a-9aec-f4f827f20cac&displaylang=en

OpenOffice.org™	This is a free word processing software. http://www.openoffice.org/
Adobe® Acrobat® X Pro	This is a commercial PDF software by Adobe®. http://www.adobe.com/products/acrobatpro/
PDF Forge®	This is free PDF software. http://www.pdfforge.org/
Cute PDF™	This is a free PDF software. http://www.cutepdf.com
Adobe® Reader® X	This software allows viewers to view PDF files if PDF software is not already installed on their computer. http://get.adobe.com/reader/?promoid=BONRM

Special Note: PDF files are a good option for online documents as the documents are securable and viewing the files is not dependent on using the software that was used to create the document. Also, some PDF software programs allow for interactive activities.

Microsoft Office PowerPoint® Presentation Software and Microsoft PowerPoint® Presentation Software Add Ins/Plug Ins

Microsoft Office PowerPoint® Presentation Software

Microsoft Office Power Point® is software for creating slide show presentations. The educator can include video, audio, hyperlinks, and some animation. There may be issues with a large file size and learners not being able to open the presentation without Microsoft Office PowerPoint® presentation software or the Microsoft PowerPoint Viewer®. This can be simply resolved by converting the files to a Flash format.

Resources For Microsoft Office PowerPoint® Presentation Software

Microsoft Office PowerPoint® Presentation Software	This is a commercial presentation software by Microsoft®. http://office.microsoft.com/en-us/powerpoint/default.aspx
Microsoft Office PowerPoint Viewer®	The free Microsoft Office PowerPoint Viewer® is needed if Microsoft Office Power Point® Presentation Software is not installed. http://www.microsoft.com/downloads/details.aspx?familyid=048DC840-14E1-467D-8DCA-19D2A8FD7485&displaylang=en

Microsoft PowerPoint® Presentation Software Add Ins/Plug Ins

There are software types that can be used in conjunction with Microsoft Office PowerPoint® presentation software and are considered Microsoft Office Power Point® presentation software add ins or plug ins. There are add ins/plug ins that allow the presentation to be converted to a flash file which significantly reduces file size and decreases some of the issues learners may have with viewing the file. There is also an add in/plug in that allows users to create and add animated talking characters to presentations. There are numerous other add ins/plug ins and resources available for use with Microsoft PowerPoint™ presentation software.

***Resources for Microsoft PowerPoint® Presentation Software Add Ins/
Plug Ins***

Camtasia®	This commercial software by TechSmith® is a screen recording software that can be used to record Microsoft Office PowerPoint® presentations. Quizzes, closed captioning, narration, audio, video, and callouts can be added to the presentation. http://www.techsmith.com/camtasia.asp
Articulate Studio®	This commercial software is used with Microsoft Office PowerPoint® presentation software to create interactive flash presentations. Quizzes, narration, audio, and video can be added to the presentation. http://www.articulate.com/products/studio.php
Adobe® Presenter®	This commercial software by Adobe® is used with Microsoft Office PowerPoint® presentation software to create interactive presentations. Quizzes, closed captioning, narration, audio, and video can be added to the presentation. http://www.adobe.com/products/presenter/
Adobe® Captivate® 5.5	This commercial software by Adobe® can be used for screen recordings and interactive presentations. Quizzes, closed captioning, narration, audio, video, and callouts can be added to the presentation. This software can also be used with Microsoft PowerPoint® presentation software. http://www.adobe.com/products/captivate/?promoid=121DJGSO_P_US_FP2_CP4_MN&tt=P_US_FP2_CP4_MN

Power Converter Pro®	This commercial software by Presentation Pro® can be used to convert Microsoft Office PowerPoint® presentations to flash video files or other file types. Quizzes, closed captioning, narration, audio, and video can be added to the presentation. http://www.presentationpro.com/power_converter_pro.aspx
Adobe® Flash® Player 11	This free software is needed to view flash files unless software allowing the viewing of flash files is already installed. http://www.adobe.com/products/flashplayer/
Vox Proxy®	This commercial software by Right Seat Software, Inc.® allows educators to create and add animated talking characters to Microsoft Office PowerPoint® presentations. The characters can be scripted to perform a variety of gestures. The voice of the characters can be scripted using text speech engines or through recorded voices. http://www.voxproxy.com/
Presentation Pro®	This company offers add ins/plug ins as well as a variety of other resources to be used in conjunction with Microsoft Power Point® presentation software. http://www.presentationpro.com/products.aspx

Graphics, Images, and Photos

Graphics, images, and photos can reinforce online content. However, large file sizes can present problems. Educators will need to compress these files types to the smallest size possible while maintaining quality. Commercial and open source resources are available for graphics, images, and photos. The educator can also produce and edit his/her own graphics, images, and photos using a digital camera and editing software.

Resources for Graphics, Images, and Photos

Multimedia Backpack®	This is commercial software by FTC Publishing® offers pictures, sounds, and videos. http://www.ftcpublishing.com/index.php?option=com_content&view=article&id=20&Itemid=56

Teacher Tap: Professional Development Resources for Educators and Librarians®	The Teacher Tap® web-site provides various resources for images and media. http://eduscapes.com/tap/topic98.htm
10 Tips for Using Graphics in e-Learning®	The Syberworks® web-site provides tips on using graphics. http://www.syberworks.com/articles/10tips_graphics.htm
Gimp: A Community-Indexed Photo Archive®	This web-site contains free photos and images to use according to fair use policy. http://gimp-savvy.com/PHOTO-ARCHIVE/
Copyright Free Photos.com®	This web-site contains free photos. http://www.copyrightfreephotos.com/
iStockphoto®	iStockphoto® offers royalty free photos, illustrations, video, and audio for purchase. http://www.istockphoto.com/index.php
Clip Art ETC®	This web-site provides free clip art for use by educators and students. http://etc.usf.edu/clipart/

Resources for Producing and Editing Graphics, Images, and Photos

Adobe Photoshop Elements™	This is a commercial software by Adobe®. http://www.adobe.com/products/photoshopelwin/
Adobe Photoshop CS4™	This is a commercial software by Adobe®. http://www.adobe.com/products/photoshop/family/prosolutions/
Gimp™	This is a free software for graphics, photos, and images. http://www.gimp.org/

Audio

Audio files can be used to supplement online content and engage the online learner. There are a variety of sound file types available. Two common file types are WAV and MP3 with the following extensions (.wav and .mp3). WAV files are large files that can be difficult to download and open. WAV files also use a lot of server space when downloaded into the course management system. MP3 files are much smaller files and are a better option for online resources. MP3 files can be recorded using a MP3 recorder or by using a computer microphone and software that allows recording of MP3 files. There are also commercial resources for sound files. Audio files may be too large to host on the institution server, so the educator may need to use an outside source for media hosting.

Resources for Audio Recording Software

Free Sound Recorder™	This is a free audio recording software. http://www.sound-recorder.biz/free_sound_recorder.html
Audacity™	This is a free audio recording software. This software also provide the capability to change existing WAV files to MP3 files. http://audacity.sourceforge.net/ Resources for Audio Files
Soundpack™	This is a commercial software for audio files by FTC Publishing®. http://www.ftcpublishing.com/index.php?option=com_content&view=article&id=27&Itemid=55
Multimedia Backpack™	This is a commercial software by FTC Publishing® offering pictures, sounds, and videos. http://www.ftcpublishing.com/index.php?option=com_content&view=article&id=20&Itemid=56

Resource for Media Hosting

Screencast.com™	Screencast.com™ provides media hosting solutions. This is a commercial product by TechSmith®. http://screencast.com/

Video

Video files can be added to online presentations and courses to provide or supplement content and engage the online learner. Video can be downloaded by users or can be streaming. Videos can be obtained from outside resources or the educator can produce and edit his/her own videos using a video camera and video editing software. Video files may be too large to host on the institution server, so the educator may need to use an outside source for media hosting.

Resources for Videos

streamingmedia.com®	The streamingmedia.com® web-site provides information on streaming and downloading video. http://www.streamingmedia.com/article.asp?id=8456&page=1
Multimedia Back-pack™	This is a commercial software by FTC Publishing® offering pictures, sounds, and videos. http://www.ftcpublishing.com/index.php?option=com_content&view=article&id=20&Itemid=56
Teacher Tap®	This link to the Teacher Tap® web-site provides various resources for images and media. http://eduscapes.com/tap/topic98.htm
YouTube®	YouTube® is a site offering video sharing. There are videos on a variety of topics. Videos must be screened for appropriateness. http://www.youtube.com/

Resources for Video Production and Editing

Camtasia™	In addition to being used to record Power Point™ slide show presentations, this commercial software by Tech-Smith® can also be used to edit videos and audio. Quizzes, closed captioning, narration, audio, and callouts can be added to the presentation. The final presentation can be exported in a variety of formats. http://www.techsmith.com/camtasia.asp
Adobe Premiere Elements™	This is a video editing commercial software by Adobe®. http://www.adobe.com/products/premiereel/

Resource for Media Hosting

Screencast.com®	Screencast.com™ provides media hosting solutions. This is a commercial product by TechSmith®. http://screencast.com/

Screen Capture and Screen Recording

Screen capture and screen recording can also be used in online courses. Screen capture and screen recording are especially helpful in "How To" tutorials. Screen capture and screen recordings are also helpful for assisting technical support with trouble shooting technical problems and error messages.

Resources for Screen Capture

Snag It™	Snag It™ is a commercial software by TechSmith® used to capture computer screen shots. Editing functions allow the user to add callouts, arrows, and others to highlight important areas. http://www.techsmith.com/screen-capture.asp
Wink™	Thisisafreescreencapturesoftwareusedforscreenshots. http://www.debugmode.com/wink/

Resources for Screen Recording

Camtasia™	In addition to being used to record Microsoft Power Point™ slide show presentations, editing video files, editing audio files, this commercial software by TechSmith® can also be used to record the user's computer screen. Quizzes, closed captioning, narration, audio, video, and callouts can be added to the presentation. The final presentation can be exported in a variety of formats. http://www.techsmith.com/camtasia.asp
CamStudio™	This is a free software used for screen recording. http://camstudio.org/

Podcasting

Podcasts can be used to provide or supplement online content and engage the online learner. A podcast is an audio file or a narrated video file that students can download to an appropriate player. Students can listen and/or view the files as often as they wish from their players at anytime. There a variety of instructional materials that can be recorded as podcasts such as lectures, informational sessions, trips, etc.

Resources for Creating Podcasts

Educause: Transforming Education Through Information Technologies®	This web-site provides links to resources and information on podcasting. http://www.educause.edu/Resources/Browse/Podcasting/17589
Free Sound Recorder™	This is a free audio recording software. http://www.sound-recorder.biz/free_sound_recorder.html

Audacity™	This is a free audio recording software. This software also provides the capability to change existing WAV files to MP3 files. http://audacity.sourceforge.net/
Camtasia™	In addition to being used to record Power Point™ slide show presentations, this commercial software by Tech-Smith® can also be used to edit videos and audio. Quizzes, closed captioning, narration, video, and callouts can be added to the presentation. The final presentation can be exported in a variety of formats. http://www.techsmith.com/camtasia.asp
Articulate Studio™	This commercial software is used with Microsoft Office Power Point™ presentation software to create interactive flash presentations. Quizzes, narration, audio, and video can be added to the presentation. Also included is the capability to edit video and change video formats. http://www.articulate.com/products/studio.php
ePodcast Creator™	This is a commercial software by Industrial Audio Soft-ware® for creating podcasts. http://www.industrialaudiosoftware.com/products/epod-castcreator.html
Juice™	Juice® is a free podcasting management software. http://juicereceiver.sourceforge.net
Screencast.com™	Screencast.com® provides media hosting solutions. This is a commercial product by TechSmith®. http://screencast.com/
YouTube®	YouTube® is a site offering video sharing. There are videos on a variety of topics. Videos must be screened for appro-priateness. http://www.youtube.com/
iTunes®	iTunes® offers podcasts. There are podcasts on a variety of topics. Podcasts must be screened for appropriateness. iTunes® also offers iTunes® U allowing schools/institutions to host password protected accounts. http://www.apple.com/itunes/whatson/podcasts/

Case-Based Instruction

The terms "case-study", "case-method", and "case-based instruction" are often used interchangeably when referring to instructional methods (Mar-sick, 1990). Ertmer and Dillon (1998) defined case-based instruction as a "teaching method that requires students to actively participate in realistic problem situations reflecting the kind of experiences typically encountered in the discipline under study" (p. 606). Malasky (1984) defined a case-study as "an oral or written account of a realistic situation, including sufficient detail to make it possible for the participants to analyze the problems involved and to determine possible solutions" (p. 9.5).

Traditional education methods focus on the students receiving information and knowledge from the teacher (Williams, 1992). Case-based instruction requires the student to identify areas that need further study and to research and find answers to questions about the case (Williams, 1992). This type of learning helps the students become familiar with solving real life problems (Williams, 1992).

Case-based instruction has many uses in education. Case-based instruction can be used to provide realistic learning situations/opportunities and to evaluate learning (Malasky, 1984). Case-based instruction can be used to promote learning beyond memorization (Delpier, 2006) and to facilitate application of concepts (Mayo, 2004). Case-based instruction can be used for facilitating transfer of learning, leadership training, ethics training, diversity training, conflict resolution training, and interpersonal skills training (Nieymer, 1995). Case-based instruction is highly used in medical, legal (Smith, 1999; Williams, 1992) teacher (Gartland & Field, 2004), psychology (Mayo, 2004), management (Nieymer, 1995; Smith, 1999) engineering, and technology (Smith, 1999) education.

There are advantages to using case-based instruction in education. Some advantages include: cases are relevant to real world situations (Malasky, 1984; Nieymer, 1995); links theory to practice (Ertmer & Dillon, 1998; Gartland & Field, 2004; Mayo, 2004; Mitchell, 2004; Smith & Diaz, 2002; Wright, 1996); can be used with the relatively inexperienced learner or advanced learners (Marsick, 1990); accommodates different learning styles (Davis & Wilcox, 2005); and case-based instruction blends well with other teaching methods (Malasky, 1984). Other advantages include: case-based instruction promotes active (Davis & Wilcox, 2005; Delpier, 2006; Kunselman & Johnson, 2004; Malasky, 1984; Mitchell, 2004), self-directed (Mayo, 2004), and cooperative (Davis & Wilcox, 2005; Gartland & Field 2004; Kunselman & Johnson, 2004; Mayo, 2004; Mitchell, 2004; Wright, 1996) learning. Case-based instruction also promotes the development of critical thinking skills necessary for the student's chosen discipline (Davis & Wilcox, 2005; Ertmer & Dillon, 1998; Kunselman & Johnson, 2004; Malasky, 1984; Mayo, 2004; Mitchell, 2004), increases student interest and motivation (Davis & Wilcox, 2005; Malasky, 1984), and promotes reflective thinking (Ertmer & Dillon, 1998; Smith & Diaz, 2002).

There are also some disadvantages to using case-based instruction. Some disadvantages include: cases can be difficult and time consuming to write, cases may become outdated, requiring periodic revision (Malasky, 1984), and lack of generalization of learning can occur if case-studies used are not diverse enough (Williams, 1992). Case-based instruction is not a good instructional strategy for learners who have decreased motivation (Ertmer & Dillon, 1998) or students who do not fully participate (Delpier, 2006).

Resources for Case-Based Instruction

University of Medicine and Dentistry of New Jersey's Online Center for Teaching Excellence®	This site has numerous links for information regarding case-based education. Topics include introduction to case-based instruction; finding, designing, and evaluating cases for teaching, teaching with cases: methods and tools; and discipline specific and interdisciplinary case repositories and examples; and additional resources on case-based learning. http://cte.umdnj.edu/active_learning/active_case.cfm
State University of New York at Buffalo's Case Studies in Science®	This is the State University of New York at Buffalo's Case Studies in Science® web-site. This site has numerous links for discipline specific case studies. http://ublib.buffalo.edu/libraries/projects/cases/webcase.htm

Animation

Animation can be used to reinforce online content and engage the online learner. Animation can be used to demonstrate activity, motion, and progression of a simulated object (Mayer & Moreno, 2002). When animation is added to narration, there is increased learning as compared to presenting materials in a narration only format, if the animation is designed appropriately (Mayer & Moreno, 2002). Animation should be directly related to instructional objectives.

Resources for Animations

Animation Library®	Animation Library® offers free animations. http://www.animationlibrary.com/
Best Animations®	Best Animations® offers free animations. http://www.bestanimations.com/
eduMedia®	eduMedia® is a commercial subscription based resource for animations and simulations. http://www.edumedia-sciences.com/en/

Resources for Creating Animations

Blender™	This is a free software for creating animations. http://www.blender.org/
Adobe® Flash CS6 Professional	This is a commercial software by Adobe. http://www.adobe.com/products/ flash/?promoid=121DJGSS_P_US_FP2_FL_CS4_ MN&tt=P_US_FP2_FL_CS4_MN
Vox Proxy™	This commercial software by Right Seat Software, Inc.® allows users to create and add animated talking characters to their Microsoft Office Power Point™ slide show presentations. The characters can be scripted to perform a variety of gestures. The voice of the characters can be scripted using text speech engines or through recorded voices. http://www.voxproxy.com/
Autodesk® Maya®	This is a commercial software by Autodesk® for creating animations. http://usa.autodesk.com/maya/

Simulation and Virtual Reality

A simulation represents a simple or complex real life situation (Jeffries, 2005; Malasky, 1984; McKeachie & Svinicki, 2006). A simulation can be used for technical demonstrations or procedures and for problem solving situations in which the participant must take appropriate actions (Jeffries, 2005; Malasky, 1984). Simulations provide immediate feedback regarding actions. Simulations offer a safe environment for learning using scenarios and role play (Hartley, 2006; Roy, Sticha, Kraus, & Olsen, 2006).

Virtual reality is a form of simulation. Virtual reality has been defined as "...a collection of technologies that allow people to interact efficiently with three-dimensional computerized databases in real time, using their natural senses and skills" (Kneebone, 2003, p. 270). Simulation and virtual reality have many uses in education. Simulation and virtual reality can be used to teach: health care/medical education (Glittenburg & Binder, 2006; Comer, 2005; Kneebone, 2003; Vernon & Peckham, 2002); procedural and technical skills (Kneebone, 2003, Malasky, 1984); e-commerce (Horton, Davenport, Hall, & Rosenbaum, 2002); management (Mitchell, 2004); conflict resolution (Elliot, Kaufmann, Gardner, & Burgess 2002); science, foreign language, and sociology (McKeachie & Svinicki, 2006); and laboratory course components (Edgar, 2005).

There are advantages to using simulation and virtual reality in education. Some advantages include: students are active participants and learn by doing

(Bernstein, Scheerhorn, & Ritter, 2002; Hartley, 2006; Horton et al., 2002; Jeffries, 2005; Kneebone & ApSimon, 2001; Malasky, 1984; McKeachie & Svinicki, 2006; Mitchell, 2004;); increases student motivation (Bernstein et al., 2002; Malasky, 1984; Mitchell, 2004;); can provide realistic learning environments (Kneebone, 2003; Malasky, 1984; Mitchell, 2004;) and allow for repeated practice of skills in a safe environment (Bernstein et al., 2002; Jeffries, 2005; Kneebone, 2003, Kneebone & ApSimon, 2001; Mitchell, 2004; Vernon & Peckham, 2002). Other advantages include: can be designed for students to receive immediate feedback (Jeffries, 2005; Shim, Brock, & Jenkins, 2005; Mitchell, 2004; Kneebone, 2003; Vernon & Peckham, 2002); promotes critical thinking and decision making skills (Comer, 2005; Jeffries, 2005; Mitchell, 2004, McKeachie & Svinicki, 2006; Shim et al., 2005); facilitates skill transfer (Mitchell, 2004); and promotes team work (Jeffries, 2005; Mitchell, 2004). Simulation and virtual reality can also promote retention and increase student interest (Vernon & Peckham, 2002).

There are some disadvantages to using simulations and virtual reality. One disadvantage is the educator may have difficulty keeping track of students (Bernstein et al., 2002). It may also be difficult to find a simulation that meets the specific needs of the course (McKeachie & Svinicki, 2006). Finally, creating original simulations can be time consuming, expensive to create, and requires technical expertise (Hartley, 2006; Malasky, 1984; McKeachie & Svinicki, 2006).

Resources for Simulation and Virtual Reality

The National Center for Simulation®	This organization provides links, information, and resources for simulation. http://www.simulationinformation.com/cms/
eduMedia®	eduMedia® is a commercial subscription based resource for animations and simulations. http://www.edumedia-sciences.com/en/

Resources for Creating Simulation and Virtual Reality

Second Life®	Second Life® is an online virtual world. http://secondlife.com/
Forio™	Forio™ offers simulations, capabilities to produce simulations, and hosting for simulations. http://forio.com/
Adobe® Director® 11.5	This commercial software by Adobe® provides capabilities for game and simulation creation. http://www.adobe.com/products/director/

Games

Games based on course content, can be fun and engaging. Games provide a supplemental method of learning course material. Games allow learners to receive immediate feedback as the games are played (Azriel, Erthal, & Starr, 2005).

Games have many uses in education. Games can be used for content review in almost any discipline (Beth & Ayotte, 2006). Games are useful in promoting leadership skills, teaching technical skills, teaching decision making skills, and promoting teamwork (Malasky, 1984). Games can also be used to evaluate learning (Malasky, 1984) and as a self-assessment tool by learners.

There are several advantages to using games in education. Games increase student interest, motivation, and participation, while promoting active learning (Azriel et al., 2005; Barab, Thomas, Dodge, Carteaux, & Tuzon, 2005; Beth & Ayotte, 2006; Malasky, 1984; Pivec & Dziabenko, 2004) and retention of knowledge (Pivec & Deziabenko, 2004). Games promote teamwork, collaborative learning, decision making, problem solving, and critical thinking skills (Azriel et al., 2005; Beth & Ayotte, 2006; Pivec & Dziabenko, 2004; Malasky, 1984). Finally, games encourage communication (Azriel et al., 2005; Beth & Ayotte, 2006).

There are some disadvantages to using games in education. Games can be time consuming to develop (Malasky, 1984). However, there are many game templates readily available now that decrease creation time. Games can be costly if purchased (Malasky, 1984). Although, that may change as more options become available.

Resources for Games and Game Creation

Adobe® Director® 11.5	This commercial software by Adobe® provides capabilities for game and simulation creation. http://www.adobe.com/products/director/
FTC Publishing®	FTC Publishing® offers several types of commercial game creation software. This is the web-site for the "Who Wants to Get Rich®" software. Games can be created and added to online courses. http://www.ftcpublishing.com/index.php?option=com_content&view=article&id=85&Itemid=127
Lee's Summit MOR-7 School District: Game Resources®	This web-site of Lee's Summit, MO R-7 School District® provides links to a variety of free online game templates and pre-made games. http://its.leesummit.k12.mo.us/gameresources.htm

Parade of Games in PowerPoint®	This web-site provides a variety of free online game templates for us in Microsoft PowerPoint® Presentation Software. http://facstaff.uww.edu/jonesd/games/index.html
Adventure Maker™	Adventure Maker® offers a free software for game creation. http://www.adventuremaker.com/overview.htm
Quia®	This repository contains a variety of online learning and teaching materials for several content areas. There are also templates for creating online activities and quizzes. Educators must register to access and use resources. http://www.quia.com/servlets/quia.web.QuiaWebManager
EclipseCrossword™	EclipseCrossword™ offers a free software for crossword puzzle creation. http://www.eclipsecrossword.com/
SoftChalk LessonBuilder™	This is a lesson or learning object creation software by SoftChalk®. Educators can add a variety of multimedia and text-based content. Educators can also create interactive activities, assessment questions, and text poppers. The lesson is packaged and delivered by electronic means. http://www.softchalk.com/

Learning Objects and Online Lessons

Learning objects are instructional materials that are combined into a reusable object or lesson (Alonso, Lopez, Manrique, & Vines, 2008; Bennett & McGee, 2005) to address instructional objective or objectives (Ruiz et al., 2006). Learning objects contain: content presented in some digital manner, methods for learner interaction, and a way to package the content and interaction (Ruiz et al., 2006). Learning objects or lessons can be delivered through a course management system, over the internet, or on a CD and can be repurposed for use in a variety of contexts (Alonso et al., 2008).

Learning objects may include a variety of multi-media, interactive activities, and assessment items. There are a variety of resources for learning objects, including learning object repositories which contain collections of learning objects in different content areas. There are also resources available for the educator to create learning objects or online lessons.

Resources for Learning Objects

MERLOT: Multimedia Educational Resource for Learning and Online Teaching®	This repository contains a variety of peer reviewed online learning and teaching materials for several content areas. Educators must register to access and use resources. http://www.merlot.org/merlot/index.htm
Wisc-Online: Wisconsin Online Resource Center®	This repository contains a variety of learning objects for several content areas. Members can also build games to include in teaching materials. Educators must register to access and use resources. http://www.wisc-online.com/
Quia®	This repository contains a variety of online learning and teaching materials for several content areas. There are also templates for creating online activities and quizzes. Educators must register and pay an annual fee to access and use resources. http://www.quia.com/servlets/quia.web.QuiaWebManager
HippoCampus®	This web-site provides resources and learning objects for a variety of subjects. http://www.hippocampus.org/
The Orange Grove: Florida's K-20 Digital Repository®	This repository contains a variety of online learning and teaching materials for several content areas. Florida educators must register to access and use resources. http://www.theorangegrove.org/
NCOR: National Repository of Online Courses®	This repository contains a variety of online learning and teaching materials for several content areas. There are academic institution and commercial vendor license available. There are also free resources available for teachers and students through the Hippocampus® division of the NCOR. http://www.montereyinstitute.org/nroc/
SAS Curriculum Pathways®	This repository contains a variety of online learning and teaching materials in several content areas. The resources are free to educators. Institutions are required to register for a subscription. http://www.sascurriculumpathways.com/
Campus Alberta Repository of Educational Objects®	This repository contains free post secondary educational objects for use by educators. http://www.ucalgary.ca/commons/careo/index.html

| Penn State: Multimedia Teaching Objects Repository® | This site contains royalty free teaching objects that can be used for educational, personal, or noncommercial purposes.
http://tlt.its.psu.edu/mto/index.html |

Resources for Learning Object and Online Lesson Creation

SoftChalk LessonBuilder®	LessonBuilder® is a lesson or learning object creation software by SoftChalk®. Educators can add a variety of multimedia and text-based content. Educators can also create interactive activities, assessment questions, and text poppers. The lesson is packaged and delivered by electronic means. http://www.softchalk.com/
Adobe Captivate 4 ™	This commercial software by Adobe® can be used for screen recordings and interactive presentations. Quizzes, closed captioning, narration, audio, video, and callouts can be added to the presentation. This software can also be used with Power Point®. The final presentation can be exported as a Flash video. http://www.adobe.com/products/captivate/?promoid=121DJGSO_P_US_FP2_CP4_MN&tt=P_US_FP2_CP4_MN
Camtasia™	In addition to being used to record Power Point™ slide show presentations, this commercial software by TechSmith® can also be used to edit videos and audio. Quizzes, closed captioning, narration, audio, and callouts can be added to the presentation. The final presentation can be exported in a variety of formats. http://www.techsmith.com/camtasia.asp

Web Quests

A web quest is a learning/teaching strategy in which learners take an active role in learning using the Internet to find information (Halat, 2008). A learner is given a task with several activities requiring the student to access online resources (Sandars, 2005). Web quests must use a structured approach to facilitate learning (Sandars, 2005).

Resource for Web Quests

| WebQuest.org® | This web-site by Bernie Dodge, PhD, Department of Educational Technology, San Diego State University provides a variety of resources for web quests.
http://webquest.org/index.php |

Papers and Projects

Online papers and projects allow learners to explore a topic in detail. Topics can be assigned by the educator or students can be allowed to pick topics of personal/professional interest related to the course subject matter. Students must research topics to complete papers and projects based on guidelines established by the instructor. Papers and projects can be completed individually or as groups. Group papers and projects will promote student-student interaction as well as student-content interaction.

Resource for Writing

The OWL at Purdue®	The Online Writing Lab (OWL)® at Purdue University provides information on a variety of topics related to writing. The resources are free for noncommercial purposes including personal, education, and training. If linking to the site, it is requested that users notify the coordinator. https://owl.english.purdue.edu/owl/resource/553/01/

Portfolios

A portfolio can be "defined as a purposeful collection of a student's work that tells a story of the student's efforts, progress, or achievement in one or more areas" (Cook–Benjamin, 2001, p. 6). Snadden and Thomas (1998) defined portfolios as "the collection of evidence that learning has taken place" (p. 192). Portfolios can be used for a single course or across a program of study (Gaide, 2006; White, 2004).

A portfolio can contain various items depending on the objectives of the portfolio. A portfolio can include student experiences, examples of completed projects, and critical reviews of journal articles that the student has read (Snadden & Thomas, 1998). A portfolio can also include workshops, conferences, or continuing education courses attended (Snadden & Thomas, 1998). In medical/health profession settings, patient experiences or critical incidents may also be included in a portfolio (Snadden & Thomas, 1998). A portfolio may have a work selection requirement (Smith & Tillema, 2003). Reflections are also a part of many portfolios (Snadden & Thomas, 1998).

Portfolios can include various methods of content presentation. Some methods of content presentation in electronic portfolios include: text; graphics; audio; and video (Canada, 2002; Challis, 1999; Gibbs, 2004; Mason, Pegler, & Weller, 2004; Snadden & Thomas, 1998). Other methods of content presentation include: references and/or links to other resources and/or web-sites; photographs; illustrations; diagrams; and charts (Canada, 2002; Challis, 1999; Mason et al., 2004). Pages can be linked together for easy navigation through each of the components (Canada, 2002). Electronic portfolios can posted on campus networks (Chang, 2001), student websites (Canada, 2002), or saved on a CD.

Portfolios can be used for developmental, presentation, and/or assessment purposes (Blair & Godsall, 2006; Mason et al., 2004). Developmental portfolios can be used to: increase self awareness (Whitsed, 2005); facilitate self-assessment (Whitsed, 2005); promote autonomy in learners (Challis, 2001); and promote development of critical thinking skills (Challis, 2001; Corcoran & Nicholson, 2004). Developmental portfolios allow a student to set his/her own goals and outcomes and measure progress (Whitsed, 2005). Developmental portfolios provide learning assessment (Corcoran & Nicholson, 2004); allow students and educator to track skills or learning over time (Snadden & Thomas, 1998; Whitsed, 2005); and link theory to practice (Challis, 1999, Corcoran & Nicholson, 2004; Snaadden & Thomas, 1998).

Presentation portfolios can be used to: promote autonomy in learners (Challis, 2001); link theory to practice (Challis, 1999; Corcoran & Nicholson, 2004; Snadden & Thomas, 1998). Presentation portfolios help facilitate continuous professional development (Corcoran & Nicholson, 2004). Presentation portfolios can be used to collect work experiences to demonstrate professional competence and specific professional experience to employers (Whitsed, 2005).

Assessment portfolios can be used for both formative and summative assessment of learning (Challis, 1999; Corcoran & Nicholson, 2004; Smith & Tillema, 2003; Snadden & Thomas, 1998). Assessment portfolios promote autonomy in learners (Challis, 2001). Assessment portfolios also promote the development of critical thinking skills (Challis, 2001; Corcoran & Nicholson, 2004).

There are several advantages to using portfolios in education. Portfolios can be used for almost any discipline or subject and customized for specific learning outcomes (White, 2004). Portfolios accommodate various learning styles (Challis, 1999); allow students to focus on goals and objectives (Gaide, 2006); and increase student motivation (Hewett, 2004). Portfolios allow students to have some control of the learning process through choice of portfolio materials to demonstrate their achievements, promote student responsibility for learning, and provide the opportunity for students to demonstrate achievement of the goals and objectives for the portfolio (Canada, 2002; Challis, 2001; Hewett, 2004; Orland–Barak, 2005; Robbins, 2006; & Wickersham & Chambers, 2006). Portfolios also foster student centered learning by engaging students in self-assessment, allowing students to identify both strengths and weaknesses, and promoting independent and active learning (Challis, 1999; Corcoran & Nicholson, 2004; Cook–Benjamin, 2001; Gibbs, 2004; Hewett, 2004; Orland–Barak, 2005; Pitts, Coles, &

Thomas, 2001; Whitsed, 2005). Portfolios encourage professional growth and development (Challis, 1999; Orland–Barak, 2005; Smith & Tillema, 2003; Snadden & Thomas, 1998). Portfolios promote reflective learning (Challis, 1999; Corcoran & Nicholson, 2004; Driessen, Tartwijk, Overeen, Vermunt, & van der Vleuten, 2005; Gaide, 2006; Hewett, 2004; Kay, 2004; Orland–Barak, 2005; Pitts et al., 2001; Snadden & Thomas, 1998; Smith & Tillema, 2003; Whitsed, 2005) and promote higher order thinking (Cook–Benjamin, 2001). Portfolios allow students to practice writing skills (Robbins, 2006); promote lifelong learning (Corcoran & Nicholson, 2004); and promote a positive attitude toward learning (Cook–Benjamin, 2001). In particular, electronic/online portfolios have several advantages. Electronic portfolios provide for easy navigation (Canada, 2002); can utilize multiple types of media (Venezky & Oney, 2004); are portable and easily assessable (Gaide, 2006; Gibbs, 2004; Robbins; 2006; Venezky & Oney, 2004); and are easy to update (Blair & Godsall, 2006; Canada, 2002; Gibbs, 2004; Mason, et al., 2004; Venezky & Oney, 2004). After the course has ended, students can continue to maintain and revise their electronic/online portfolio to demonstrate professional work for future academic or career pursuits (Canada, 2002; Hewett, 2004). Finally, posting electronic portfolios online accesses a larger audience (Gaide, 2006; Gibbs, 2004).

There are some disadvantages to using portfolios in education. Students may resist the use of portfolios, especially if students do not feel prepared (Challis, 2001) or do not understand the portfolio concept (Carraccio & Englander, 2004). Portfolios may lead to high levels of anxiety in students (Corcoran & Nicholson, 2004), especially in regards to sharing personal feelings (Snadden & Thomas, 1998). Students may find the portfolio process excessively time consuming (Carraccio & Englander, 2004; Corcoran & Nicholson, 2004). Portfolios may also be time consuming for educators (Gibbs, 2004). Portfolios may be difficult to assess (Pitts et al., 2001) and students may have issues with the technology (Wickersham & Chambers, 2006).

Resources for Portfolio Development

Educause: e-portfolios-124 Resources®	This web-site provides links to resources and information on portfolios. http://www.educause.edu/Resources/Browse/eportfolios/17180
Aurbach and Associates, Inc.®	Aurbach and Associates, Inc.® offers various tools for portfolio development and journaling for students and educators. http://www.aurbach.com/

| Pupil Pages® | Pupil Pages® offers tools for portfolio development and management for students and educators.
http://www.pupilpages.com/ |

Journals

Journals can help learners "...describe, interpret, and analyze their learning experiences and perspectives" (Gillis, 2001, p. 50). Journaling can focus on various aspects of the learning experience. For example, students can be asked to reflect on how the content learned can be applied to their personal and/or professional lives.

Journal writing has several uses in education. Journal writing can be used in almost any discipline (Hubbs & Brand, 2005). Journal writing can be used for professional (Boud, 2001; Hubbs & Brand, 2005; Heimstra, 2001) and personal development (Jarvis, 2001). Journal writing can be used to provide a record of learning to address continuing competence issues in health care (Gillis, 2001). Journal writing can also be used for notes and reflection during research (Jarvis, 2001).

There are advantages to using journal writing in education. Journal writing promotes reflective and active learning through all learning stages (Bolin, Khramtsova, & Saarnio, 2005; Boud, 2001; Heimstra, 2001; Hubbs & Brand, 2005; Jarvis, 2001). Through reflection, journal writing allows for self discovery and personal insight (Hubbs & Brand, 2005; Hampton & Morrow; 2003 Heimstra, 2001) and helps students understand how they learn (Boud, 2001). Journal writing promotes critical thinking skills (Hubbs & Brand, 2005; Boud, 2001; Heimstra, 2001); problem solving skills (Heimstra, 2001); accountability (Gillis, 2001); learning in the affective domain (Bolin et al., 2005) and motivation, interest in, and understanding of the subject matter (Hampton & Morrow, 2003; Hubbs & Brand, 2005). Journal writing promotes growth in professional practice (Boud, 2001) by helping students evaluate if practice is consistent or inconsistent with theories for the subject matter (Bolin et al., 2005; Jarvis, 2001).

There are some disadvantages to using journal writing in education. Some students may feel threatened or intimidated by journal writing (English & Gillen, 2001; Jarvis, 2001). Another disadvantage is journal writing can be time consuming (Jarvis, 2001).

Online Resources

In an online course, it is important for the educator to provide links to supplemental resources. There are many valuable online resources that can be used to promote student learning. The educator, must screen online resources for appropriateness and accuracy.

Online Resources on Evaluating Information Found on the Internet

Johns Hopkins University Sheridan Libraries®	This link is for the Sheridan Libraries® at Johns Hopkins University's "Evaluating Information Found On The Internet". This resource provides valuable information on this topic. There are also links to other resources. http://www.library.jhu.edu/researchhelp/general/evaluating/
UC Berkeley Library®	This link is for the UC Berkeley Library's "Evaluating Web Pages." This resource provides valuable information on this topic. There are also links to other resources. http://www.lib.berkeley.edu/TeachingLib/Guides/Internet/Evaluate.html
The OWL at Purdue®	The Online Writing Lab (OWL)® at Purdue University provides information on a variety of topics related to writing. The resources are free for noncommercial purposes including personal, education, and training. If linking to the site, it is requested that users notify the coordinator. https://owl.english.purdue.edu/owl/resource/553/01/
Pennsylvania State University®	This is the web-site for the Pennsylvania State University's "How to Evaluate Information on the Web"®. This resources provides valuable information on this topic. http://www.libraries.psu.edu/instruction/infolit/andyou/mod6/eval.htm

Online Resources by Discipline

Allied Health Resource	UConn Health Center: The Connecticut Tutorials® This web-site provides videos for clinical examinations for the allied health/medical student. http://www.conntutorials.com/
Anatomy Resources	Get Body Smart® This web-site provides interactive activities for the system of the body. http://www.getbodysmart.com/index.htm Human Anatomy Online® This web-site provides interactive activities for the system of the body. http://www.innerbody.com/htm/body.html

	University of Minnesota Web Anatomy® This web-site provides interactive activities for the system of the body. http://msjensen.cehd.umn.edu/webanatomy/
	The Virtual Body® This web-site provides interactive activities on the brain, the skeleton, the human heart, and the digestive tract. www.medtropolis.com/VBody.asp
Biology Re-sources	zeroBio® This web-site provides interactive games, puzzles, and quizzes designed for high school science and biology students. http://www.zerobio.com/
	Biology in Motion® This web-site provides a variety of online resources for high school biology. http://biologyinmotion.com/
	BioEd Online® This web-site provides biology resources. http://www.bioedonline.org/
	Weblinks/Science/Biology/Genetics® This web-site provides a variety of links for science, biology, and genetics. http://weblearn.sheffcol.ac.uk/links/Science/Biology/Genetics/
English Resource	The OWL at Purdue® The Online Writing Lab (OWL)® at Purdue University provides a variety of topics related to writing. The resources are free for noncommercial purposes including personal, education, and training. If linking to the site, it is requested that users notify the coordinator. https://owl.english.purdue.edu/owl/resource/553/01/
Math Resources	Onlinelearning.com (Algebra Help)® This web-site provides online algebra lessons and worksheets. http://www.onlinemathlearning.com/algebra-help.html
	Mathwords.com® This web-site provides terms and formulas for algebra and calculus. http://www.mathwords.com/

Understanding Algebra® This is an online algebra book authored by James Brennan. http://www.jamesbrennan.org/algebra/
Home School Math® This web-site provides links to a variety of algebra resources. http://www.homeschoolmath.net/math_resources_4.php

Additional Instructional Resources

Southern Regional Education Board: Evalutech®	This web-site provides links to instructional resources in a variety of content areas. http://www.evalutech.sreb.org/InstResources/index.asp
Center for Research on Learning and Teaching®	This web-site provides information on online teaching strategies and resources. http://www.crlt.umich.edu/tstrategies/teachings.php
Teaching Tips Index®	This web-site provides links to a variety of resources for educators. http://honolulu.hawaii.edu/intranet/committees/FacDevCom/guidebk/teachtip/teachtip.htm
Active Learning Online: Strategies for the Online Course®	This web-site provides online course teaching strategies. http://www.acu.edu/cte/activelearning/online_main.htm
UTTelecampus: Online Education from University of Texas System Institutions®	This web-site provides links to a variety of information on online course development. http://telecampus.utsystem.edu/facultyresources/coursedevelopment/cdresources.aspx
Virginia Tech: Design Shop: Lessons in Effective Teaching®	This web-site provides information related to online education. http://www.edtech.vt.edu/edtech/id/index.html

PART II: STUDENT-STUDENT INTERACTION

Student-student interaction and collaboration are important in online education (Cox & Cox, 2008; Martinez, 2004). Student-student interaction occurs between two or more learners. Students share information and ideas and may work together to solve problems or issues. The second part of this chapter includes information on the following topics: online discussions; group learning; peer teaching; role play; blogs; wikis; and chats.

Online Discussions

Online discussions are one method of student-student interaction in the online environment. Online discussions provide an opportunity for student-student interaction through a learning community and require the learner to be an active participant in the learning process (Baglione & Nastanski, 2007; Cox & Cox, 2008; Im & Lee, 2003; Li, 2004; Schwartzman, 2006). Discussions have many uses in online education. Discussions are used for further exploration of course topics. Discussions can be used in conjunction with case-based instruction to review cases (Malasky, 1984). Discussions can be used for group work and projects (Malasky, 1984). Discussions can also be used for problem solving by having learners engage in discussion for each step of the problem (Merrill & Gilbert, 2008; Schwartzman, 2006).

In online discussions, an educator can post a question related to the content for students to discuss. Students post a response to the discussion question following the instructions and criteria posted by the educator (Cox & Cox, 2008; Schwartzman, 2006). Students then respond to other students' initial postings forming a threaded discussion. The educator monitors and facilitates the discussion (Malasky, 1984; Schwartzman, 2006)

There are advantages to using discussion in online education. Online discussions require active participation, promote interaction (Baglione & Nastanski, 2007; Cox & Cox, 2008; Im & Lee, 2003; Li, 2004; Malasky, 1984; Merrill & Gilbert, 2008; Schwartzman, 2006), promote collaboration (Cox & Cox, 2008; Li, 2004; Martinez, 2004; McLoughlin & Mynard, 2009), promote higher order thinking (McLoughlin & Mynard, 2009) and promote critical thinking (Baglione & Nastanski, 2007; Fung, 2004; Li, 2004). Online discussions allow learners to explore topics from multiple perspectives and benefit from the knowledge of other learners (Baglione & Nastanski, 2007; Fung, 2004; Im & Lee, 2003; Malasky, 1984; Wang, 2005). Online discussions may enhance cognitive development (Im & Lee, 2003), promote creativity (Li, 2004); allow time for reflection (Baglione & Nastanski, 2007; Im & Lee, 2003; Li, 2004; Lin & Overbaugh, 2007; Schwartzman, 2006; Wang, 2005); and allow for more in depth discussions than the traditional classroom (Schwartzman, 2006). Learners who may not normally participate due to shyness may find this a less threatening environment than the regular classroom to participate in discussions (McLoughlin & Mynard, 2009). Other advantages to online discussion include: students are not required to be online at the same time (Baglione & Nastanski, 2007; Cox & Cox, 2008; Fung, 2004; Li, 2004; Lin & Overbaugh, 2007; Schwartzman,

2006); students participation can be monitored (Schwartzman, 2006); and students can return to online discussions at any time to review (Baglione & Nastanski, 2007; Li, 2004).

There are some disadvantages to using online discussion. Learners may not stay focused on questions and it may be difficult for the educator to redirect. Some learners may experience information overload (Schwartzman, 2006). Some learners may dominate the discussion (Baglione & Nastanski, 2007; Li, 2004; Malasky, 1984). Another disadvantage to using online discussions is that online discussions can be time consuming to moderate, facilitate (Malasky, 1984), and grade. Some of these issues can be decreased or eliminated with proper course implementation.

Strategies for Course Implementation

1. When adding discussions to an online course it is important for the educator to establish clear discussion board instructions, guidelines, and grading rubric(s). Instructions and criteria for discussion board postings can include items such as: number of postings, length, grammar, references, replying to other students, etc. (Li, 2004). Schwartzman (2006) recommended that educators set a maximum number of postings each student can post on the discussion board to keep the discussion more manageable. Educators should also have the initial posting requirement due earlier in the assignment period than the replies, so students have the opportunity to read and respond to other student's and the instructor's postings. The educator should also identify his/her role in the online discussions. Educators may want to consider posting model posts (Schwartzman, 2006) and examples (Li, 2004). Netiquette should also be addressed in the course (Baglione & Nastanski, 2007; Li, 2004) prior to the first discussion assignment.

2. Keep discussion board groups to a manageable size. Li (2004) recommended online discussion groups of no more than 15 participants.

3. To help facilitate the building of a learning community, online courses should always have an introduction discussion (Li, 2004). The introduction discussion board also allows the learner to become familiar with posting on the discussion board.

4. Develop course discussion questions to allow further exploration of course content.

5. The educator should moderate and facilitate course discussions (Li, 2004). Educators should delete or hide inappropriate messages (Li, 2004). If the educator deletes a posting, the educator should be sure to have a screen shot of the posting for documentation and

follow-up with the student posting inappropriate messages. Educators should check the institution's policies on deleting student postings.
6.   Encourage students to compose postings using word processing software and then post online (Li, 2004). This allows the student to have a permanent copy of his/her work. This also helps prevent any loss of work due to technical problems (Li, 2004).
7.   The educator may want to consider having other types of online discussions in the class other than those directly related to course content. A student lounge discussion board may be useful for building community (Li, 2004). Having a "Questions for the Instructor" type discussion board allows the instructor to answer questions posted by students. It also allows students to post answers to the questions if appropriate, further enhancing the learning community. Students can review this discussion board before posting a question to see if the question has already been answered.

Group Learning

Group learning is another method of incorporating student-student interaction in an online course (Graham, 2002; Thompson & Ku, 2006). Group learning requires the forming of learning communities, an important component of online education (Tu & Corry, 2002). Group learning can include cooperative learning and/or collaborative learning (Graham, 2002; Paulus, 2005; Riley & Anderson, 2006). In cooperative learning tasks, each group member completes a portion of the assignment individually (Paulus, 2005). Collaboration involves group members working and collaborating on a task together (Paulus, 2005). Group learning can include "… seminar-style presentations and discussions, debates, group projects, simulations, role-play exercises, and the collaborative composition of essays, exam questions, stories, and research plans" (Tu & Corry, 2002, p. 214). Tutty and Klein (2008) also identified "…problem-based instruction; guided design; writing groups; peer teaching; workshops; discussion groups…" (p. 102) as methods of incorporating group learning.

There are advantages to using group learning in online education. Group learning allows learners to benefit from the knowledge and perspectives of other learners (McConnell, 2005, Riley & Anderson, 2006; Paulus, 2005; Thompson & Ku, 2006; Tu & Corry, 2002; Tutty & Klein, 2008). Group learning promotes problem solving skills, social skills, and self-esteem (Tutty & Klein, 2008). Group learning promotes critical thinking skills (McConnell, 2005), facilitates communication skills (McConnell, 2005; Thompson & Ku, 2006; Tutty & Klein, 2008), promotes higher achievement (Riley & Anderson, 2006), and promotes higher order thinking (Riley & Anderson, 2006; Thompson & Ku, 2006; Tutty & Klein, 2008). Group learning can also decrease student procrastination (Thompson & Ku, 2006). Finally, group learning promotes collaboration, active participation, and interaction.

There are some disadvantages to using group learning in online education. Some learners may have limited participation in their respective groups (Graham, 2002; Hasler–Waters & Napier, 2002; Thompson & Ku, 2006). Some learners may dominate the group (Hasler–Waters & Napier, 2002). Group learning is not suitable for all learners. The maturity level of the student is an important factor to consider (Hasler–Waters & Napier, 2002). Groups may not communicate effectively (Thompson & Ku, 2006). Some learners may find group work frustrating and be resistant to the process (Hasler–Waters & Napier, 2002; Thompson & Ku, 2006). Some of these issues can be decreased or eliminated with proper course implementation.

Strategies for Course Implementation

There are four elements necessary for successful learning groups:

1. Creating Groups and Opportunities for Engagement (Graham, 2002; Tu & Corry, 2002): When creating groups, keep the group size small and manageable (Graham, 2002). Depending on the intended outcomes of the group learning activity, the educator can assign learners with similar backgrounds and skills to groups or the educator can assign learners with varied backgrounds and skills to groups. Allow time for group members to become acquainted and build rapport (Hasler–Waters & Napier, 2002). Groups should establish the processes for communication and assignment completion (Graham, 2002; Hasler–Waters & Napier, 2002).

2. Structuring Learning Activities (Graham, 2002): When structuring learning activities, Graham (2002) recommended to have tasks that require different levels of skills to complete in order to facilitate participation and cooperation of all group members. Provide learners an easy method of communication within their groups like discussion boards and chat rooms.

3. Student interaction and Educator Moderation (Graham, 2002, Tu & Corry, 2002): Student interaction and educator moderation is crucial to group success (Hasler–Waters & Napier, 2002; Riley & Anderson, 2006; Tutty & Klein, 2008). More experienced group members can serve as moderators and facilitators of group work (Tu & Corry, 2002). Educators should help learners develop cooperative skills including: decision making, consensus building, dealing with conflict, basic communication, and group processing/management (Graham, 2002: Hasler–Waters & Napier, 2002). Educator feedback is important (Riley & Anderson, 2006) and should be provided timely.

4. Assessment: Establish clear expectations and guidelines for group interaction, participation, and grading (Hasler–Waters & Napier, 2002; Paulus, 2005) and include a corresponding grading rubric. Graham (2002) recommended that both group and individual accountability be elements of assessment. Thompson and Ku (2006) recommended that peer evaluation and self evaluation be included in the assessment of group learning. The educator should also have methods in place for groups to report members who are not participating (Thompson & Ku, 2006).

Peer Teaching

Peer teaching is another method of incorporating student-student interaction in an online course. In peer teaching, a student teaches other students in the course (Merrill & Gilbert, 2008; Parr, Wilson, Godinho, & Longaretti, 2004). In peer teaching, both the peer teacher and the student can benefit from the peer teaching process. Preparing the peer teaching materials and activities, as well as the process of teaching, facilitates learning for the peer teacher (Parr et al., 2004; Tang, Hernandez, & Adams, 2004). The learners gain knowledge and ideas from the peer teacher (Parr et al., 2004). Peer teaching can be used for various types of education and for a variety of learners (Parr et al., 2004).

There are advantages to using peer teaching in online education. Parr et al. (2004) identified the following advantages for peer teaching: improved learning outcomes; increased student autonomy; promotes team work; and collaboration with peers allows students to gain a variety of perspectives. Iwasiw & Goldenberg (1993) identified the following advantages for peer teaching: increases creativity; promotes responsibility; promotes interpersonal growth; and promotes accountability. Other advantages cited in the literature include: increased motivation; promotes active learning (Merrill & Gilbert, 2008; Parr et al., 2004); increased communication skills (Iwasiw & Goldenberg, 1993; Parr et al., 2004); and peer teaching prepares students for future work environments (Merrill & Gilbert, 2008).

There are some disadvantages to using peer teaching in online education. First of all, some students are not prepared to participate in the peer teaching process in the educator role. Also, some students may not be receptive to being taught by their peers (Parr et al., 2004). Peer teaching works best with mature learners. Accuracy of student teaching materials may be an issue. Educators should monitor student's materials closely. Parr et al. (2004) also identified the following disadvantages for peer teaching: group conflict may arise; possible decreased individual accountability; increased time commitment from students; some students may have more participation than others; may be difficult to assess; students may have information overload. Some of these issues can be decreased or eliminated with proper course implementation.

Strategies for Course Implementation

1. Communicate clear expectations, structure, and rubrics (Merrill & Gilbert, 2008; Parr et al., 2004).
2. Support learners in the peer teaching process and teach them how to work together (Merrill & Gilbert, 2008; Parr et al., 2004).
3. Establish level of educator intervention (Parr et al., 2004).
4. Peer teaching can be used in conjunction with other strategies such as group work, problem-based instruction (Merrill & Gilbert, 2008), discussion, and demonstration.
5. Include reflection (Parr et al., 2004) and self-assessment.
6. Include peer assessment.
7. Include formal assessment (Parr et al., 2004).

Role Play

Role play is another method of incorporating student-student interaction in an online course. In role play, teachers design a scenario in which students play roles or characters (Mercado, 2000). Educators give students a description of the scenario and characters. There can be any number of characters in the role play activity depending on the situation and learning outcomes (Mercado, 2000). The educator may assign roles or allow student choice.

Role play can be used for various types of education. It is especially useful in medical, law, ethics, and communication education. Mercado (2000) indicated role play works for "...any course dealing with human activities and interaction" (p. 117). Malasky (1984) indicated that role play is useful to practice skills learned in such areas as problem solving, counseling, and interviewing.

There are advantages to using role play in online education. Role play promotes active learning (Childress & Braswell, 2006; Mercado, 2000). Role play provides realistic learning experiences (Childress & Braswell, 2006; Lebaron & Miller, 2005; Malasky, 1984; Mercado, 2000) that promote skills that can be transferred to future real world situations (Mercado, 2000). Role play allows students to express themselves and promotes creativity (Mercado, 2000). Students learn from each other (Lebaron & Miller, 2005), experiencing learning from a variety of perspectives (Malasky, 1984). Role play also promotes communication and leadership skills (Mercado, 2000; Wentland, 2004). Role play also stimulates student interest, increases satisfaction, and promotes understanding of concepts (McCarthy & Anderson, 2000). Finally, role play improves decision making skills and critical thinking skills (Childress & Braswell, 2006; Lebaron & Miller, 2005; Wentland, 2004).

There are some disadvantages to using role play in online education. Role play scenarios can be difficult to develop (Malasky, 1984). Some students may not be prepared to participate in role play activities. Some students may not be receptive to role play and role play may create anxiety for some students (Mercado, 2000). Role play may be time consuming for educators and students (Malasky, 1984; Wentland, 2004). The management (Mercado, 2000) and assessment of role play activities may be difficult. Some of these issues can be decreased or eliminated with proper course implementation.

Strategies for Course Implementation

1. Give appropriate background information for the role play activity (Lebaron & Miller, 2005). Communicate clear expectations, structure, instructions, and rubrics ((Lebaron & Miller, 2005; Mercado, 2000) being careful not to put too many restrictions to allow learners some flexibility in the direction they can take the assignment (Lebaron & Miller, 2005). Clarify how much freedom the learners have in the role play activity (Mercado, 2000).
2. Educators should provide support and feedback (Mercado, 2000).
3. Allow sufficient time for role play activities (Lebaron & Miller, 2005).
4. Include reflection (Mercado, 2000) and self-assessment.
5. Include peer assessment.
6. Include formal assessment.

Blogs

Blogs are another method of incorporating student-student interaction in an online course. Blogs have been defined in the literature as: online conversations or diaries (Boulos & Wheeler, 2007; Dearstyne, 2005; Richardson, 2006) and online journals (Boulos & Wheeler, 2007; Dearstyne, 2005; Nakerud & Scaletta, 2008). Blogs can include text, audio, graphics, images, and/or video (Black 2006; Columbo & Columbo, 2007).

The author of the blog has control of the content (Black, 2006). The author posts his/her thoughts and ideas about topics online (Davis &Mc-Grail, 2009; Dearstyne, 2005). Some blogs only allow the specified authors to post, while other blogs allow reader comments. Blogs can be open for only selected participants or for anyone (Dearstyne, 2005).

There are advantages to using blogs in online education. Blogs are easy to set-up and use, requiring minimal technical skills (Black, 2006; Boulos & Wheeler, 2007; Dearstyne, 2005; Nakerud & Scaletta, 2008; West, Wright,

Gabbitas, & Graham, 2006). Some course management systems have built in blogging capabilities. Blogs provide new and current information on topics derived from participants' personal experience, educational background, or professional experience (Dearstyne, 2005; Mason, 2006; Wang & Hsu, 2008; West et al., 2006). The sharing of information increases student interest for the topic (Black, 2006), promotes understanding of concepts (Black, 2006; Columbo & Columbo, 2007; West et al., 2006) promotes exploration of topics; and establishes learning communities (Davis & McGrail, 2009; Sturgeon, 2008; Wang & Hsua, 2008). Learning is promoted through cooperation and collaboration (Black, 2006; Dearstyne, 2005; Ducate & Lomicka, 2008; Wang & Hsua, 2008; West et al., 2006).

There are additional advantages to using blogs in online education. Blogs promote creativity, self expression (Davis & McGrail, 2009; Dearstyne 2005; Ducate & Lomicka, 2008), self-directed learning (Mason, 2006), and reflection (Beldarrain, 2006; Black, 2006; Davis & McGrail, 2009; Ducate & Lomicka, 2008; West et al., 2006). Blogs increase the amount of time students spend learning about topics (Columbo & Columbo, 2007). Blogging promotes active learning (Ducate & Lomicka, 2008) and critical thinking (Black, 2006; Ducate & Lomicka, 2008; Richardson, 2006).

There are also disadvantages to using blogs in online education. Students may not be prepared for blogging. Blogs can be difficult to monitor/ manage and require increased time for the educator and student (Wang & Hsua, 2008). Students may resist using blogs for educational purposes. Users may make inappropriate comments (Chuang, 2008) and/or post poor quality blogs (Wang & Hsua, 2008). Some of these issues can be decreased or eliminated with proper course implementation.

Strategies for Course Implementation

1. Before implementing blogs into a course, the educator should verify the institution's policy on using blogs.
2. Use simple to use tools, preferably the blogging tools provided by the course management system. If these tools do not meet the educator's needs, the educator should be sure to use a blogging site that is appropriate for educational purposes.
3. Educate students on internet safety (Davis & McGrail, 2009), expected conduct, and netiquette (Sturgeon, 2008) Students should protect their privacy and the privacy of others (Nakerud & Scaletta, 2008). This becomes increasingly important if a blog is open for participation by others outside of the classroom and institution.
4. Have students sign a code of conduct (Sturgeon, 2008).

5. Clearly communicate the purpose of the blog as well as expectations, structure, instructions, and rubrics (Gustafson, 2008; Nakerud & Scaletta, 2008).
6. Provide support, guidance, and training (Wang & Hsua, 2008).
7. To facilitate easy navigation, organize blogs by topic (Sturgeon, 2008).
8. Depending on the level of student, educators should have an approval system for postings before students postings can go live (Gustafson, 2008), especially if blogging is done outside of the course management system.
9. Encourage peer comments for blogs (Mason, 2006).
10. The educator can have teachers, topic experts in the field of study, students enrolled in the class, other students outside of the class, and student mentors to participate in the blog (Davis & McGrail, 2009).

Resources for Educational Blogs

Course Management System Blogging Tools	The educator should determine if the institution's course management system offers appropriate blogging tools.
Class Blogmeister®	This resource offers resources for educational blogs. http://classblogmeister.com/index.php
21Classes Cooperative Learning®	This resource offers free and paid options for educational blogs. http://www.21classes.com/

Wikis

Wikis are another method of incorporating student-student interaction in an online course. A wiki allows content to be posted by an author or authors and can be edited by anyone with access to the wiki (Beldarrain, 2006; Bisoux, 2008; Boulos & Wheeler, 2007; Butcher & Taylor, 2008; Knoble & Lankshear, 2009: Minocha & Thomas, 2007; Morgan & Smith, 2008; Sanders, 2007; Skiba, 2005). Wikis may be open to the public or access can be limited (Butcher & Taylor, 2008; Engstrom & Jewett, 2005; Sanders, 2007). Most wiki software provides editing history so changes can be tracked and pages can be restored to previous versions (Beldarrain, 2006; Bisoux, 2008; Butcher & Taylor, 2008; Engstrom & Jewett, 2005; Minocha & Thomas, 2007; Morgan & Smith, 2008; Wheeler, Yeomans, & Wheeler, 2008). Wikis are typically organized by content, contain links to other information, and are searchable (Beldarrain, 2006; Engstrom & Jewett, 2005; Knoble & Lankshear, 2009; Morgan & Smith, 2008).

There are advantages to using wikis in education. Wikis promote interaction (Beldarrain, 2006; Butcher &Taylor, 2008; Minocha & Thomas, 200; Sanders, 2007; Skiba, 2005) and promote reflection (Sanders, 2007). Wikis promote collaboration (Beldarrain, 2006; Bisoux, 2008; Butcher & Taylor, 2008; Engstrom & Jewett, 2005; Knoble & Lankshear, 2009; Minocha & Thomas, 2007; Morgan & Smith, 2008; Sanders, 2007; Sheehy, 2008; Wheeler, et al., 2008) and promote learning communities (Sanders, 2007; Skiba, 2005; Wheeler et al., 2008). Wikis promote critical thinking skills (Wheeler et al., 2008). Wikis allow students to share knowledge and view topics from multiple perspectives (Boulos & Wheeler, 2007; Engstrom & Jewett, 2005; Minocha & Thomas, 2007; Skiba, 2005; Wheeler et al., 2008).

There are additional advantages to using wikis in education. Wikis are relatively easy to write (Butcher & Taylor, 2008; Knoble & Lankshear, 2009; Morgan & Smith, 2008; Sheehy, 2008; Skiba, 2005; Wheeler et al., 2008). Updates and revisions to wikis can be made timely (Butcher & Taylor, 2008; Sheehy, 2008; Skiba, 2005; Wheeler et al., 2008). Some course management systems have built in wiki tools.

There are also disadvantages to using wikis in education. Some students may not be prepared for the wiki process. Some students may be resistant to using wikis for educational purposes. Some students may have more participation than others (Wheeler et al., 2008). Wikis can be difficult to organize and tracking students work can be difficult (Skiba, 2005). Accuracy of wiki content may be an issue in some cases (Wheeler et al., 2008).

There are additional disadvantages to using wikis in education. Some wikis may lack multimedia elements (Skiba, 2005). Only one user at a time can edit a wiki page (Engstrom & Jewett, 2005; Sheehy, 2008; Wheeler et al., 2008). Some students may have a problem relinquishing ownership of their writing to allow others to edit and change (Skiba, 2005; Wheeler et al., 2008).

Strategies for Course Implementation

1. Before implementing wikis into a course, educators should verify the institution's policy on using wikis.
2. Use simple to use tools, preferably the wiki tools provided by the course management system. If these tools do not meet the educator's needs, be sure to use a wiki site that is appropriate for educational purposes.
3. Educate students on internet safety, expected conduct, and netiquette. Students should protect their privacy and the privacy of others. This becomes increasingly important if a wiki is open for participation by others outside the classroom and institution.
4. Have students sign a code of conduct.

5. Communicate the purpose of the wiki, as well as expectations, structure, instructions, and rubrics.
6. Create wiki template pages (Sheehy, 2008).
7. Require correct grammar and spelling for wiki entries (Butcher & Taylor, 2008).
8. Require that wiki entries be supported with references (Butcher & Taylor, 2008).
9. Provide support, guidance, and training (Bisoux, 2008; Wheeler et al., 2008).
10. Require active participation in the wiki (Butcher &Taylor, 2008; Wheeler et al., 2008).

Resources for Educational Wikis

Course Management System Wiki Tools	The educator should determine if the institution's course management system offers appropriate wiki tools.
Wiki Spaces®	Wiki Spaces® offers wiki tools for business and educational institutions. There is a free option available as well as subscription based options. http://www.wikispaces.com/
Wikis in Education®	Wikis in Education® by Wet Paint® offers wiki tools. Education wikis can qualify for ad free status. http://wikisineducation.wetpaint.com/

Chats

Chats are another method to incorporate student-student interaction in an online course. Chats are online discussions. Chats differ from discussion boards in that the chat sessions are synchronous with all participants online at the same time. Chats can be used to discuss specific topics as directed by the educator or can be open for student(s) to direct the chat session.

There are advantages to using chats in education. Chats promote interaction, collaboration, engagement, and reflection (Wang, 2005). Chats also promote community (Cox, Carr, & Hall, 2004; Wang, 2005). Students are able to explore topics from multiple perspectives (Wang, 2005). Chats also allow guest speakers to participate in an online course (Hines & Pearl, 2004). Some course management systems have built in chat tools.

There are also disadvantages to using chats in education. All chat participants must be online at the same time (Hines & Pearl, 2004). Students may have varied participation in the chat. Some students may dominate the chat session and some may have very limited participation (Bober & Dennen, 2001). Online chats may be difficult to manage and follow (Bober &

Dennen, 2001; Hines & Pearl, 2004; Wang, 2005). It may be difficult to keep participants on topic.

Strategies for Course Implementation

1. Verify any institution policies pertaining to chats, especially in regards to having guests participate in the chats.
2. Can have educators, topic experts in the field of study, students enrolled in the class, other students outside of the class, and student mentors to participate in the chat.
3. Use simple to use tools.
4. Educate students on internet safety, expected conduct, and netiquette. Students should protect their privacy and the privacy of others.
5. Have students sign a code of conduct.
6. Communicate the purpose of the chat, as well as expectations, structure, instructions, and rubrics (Wang, 2005).
7. Provide support, guidance, and training.
8. Require participation.
9. Start a chat session with a question (Cox et al., 2004; Wang, 2005).
10. Hines and Pearl (2004) suggested having a system for participants to indicate when they have a question or want to make a point so the educator can call on them instead of students just typing in questions and comments. The symbols used by the authors were "?" used when the participant needs to ask a question and "!" used when the participant wants to make a point (Hines & Pearl, 2004). This could help with management and flow of conversation. Software for chats may have symbols for "hand raising" built in.
11. Provide facilitation as needed.

Resources for Educational Chats

Course Management System Chat Tools	The institution's course management system may offer appropriate chat tools. These chat tools offer security for the chats. The chats can also be archived for review later and for students who could not attend the scheduled chat session.
Other	There are also many commercial and free resources available for chats, video conferencing, and/or video chats.

Special Note: Videoconferencing can also be used to conduct online discussions, lectures, and office hours. Some course management systems have integrated videoconferencing capabilities.

PART III: STUDENT-EDUCATOR INTERACTION

The interaction between the educator and the student is crucial in the online course. Educator interaction should occur before, during, and after instruction (Hirumi, 2002). Hirumi (2002) indicated the purposes of educator interaction as: "… to establish learning outcomes/objectives; to provide timely and appropriate feedback; to facilitate information presentation; to monitor and evaluate student performance; to provide (facilitate) learning activities; to initiate; maintain, and facilitate discussions; and to determine learning needs and preferences" (p. 145). The final part of this chapter includes information on the following topics: educator interaction before instruction; educator interaction during instruction; and educator interaction after instruction. Educator interaction after instruction will also address the topics of best practices for providing feedback and characteristics of effective feedback.

Educator Interaction Before Instruction

Types of educator interaction that should occur before instruction include: establishment and posting of course polices; posting important course documents; and posting the course schedule and assignment due dates. Educator interaction should also include the development of online orientations, tutorials, and ice breaker assignments. The educator should ensure all assignments have clear instructions and guidelines. Grading rubrics should be developed (Bonnel, 2008) and posted before the class starts.

One of the first types of educator interaction that should occur in an online course is the posting of a welcome message. The welcome message should include getting started information and adds a personal touch to the course (Johnson & Aragon, 2003). This is an important component of online education (Bonnel, 2008; Weiss, 2000). The welcome message or the syllabus should also include specific information regarding the educator's policy on feedback, grading, response to course e-mail, and educator participation in discussions. The educator should provide students with his/her biography (Weiss, 2000).

Educator Interaction During Instruction

Student-educator interaction, during or as part of instruction, can occur through various methods in an online course. Several methods for student-student interaction were discussed in part two of this chapter. The following methods of student-student interaction previously discussed may also be used as methods of student-educator interaction: online discussion; role play; blogs; wikis; chats, and video conferencing. Educators should take an active role in the discussion process, being sure to facilitate and engage in discussions as appropriate (Johnson & Aragon, 2003; Sitzman & Leners, 2006). When facilitating and engaging in discussions, educators should model appropriate interaction (Weiss, 2000) and be careful not to dominate the discussion. Educators can have varying degrees of participation in role play, blogs, wikis, chats, and video conferencing depending on the learning outcomes of the activity.

In addition to these previously discussed methods, educators should also send regular course messages/e-mails and/or post regular course announcements. Course messages/e-mails can be used to provide individual student feedback. Educators should also provide opportunities for immediate student feedback though self-assessment activities while students are learning concepts (Bonnel, 2008; Brookhart, 2008). These activities should have the feedback built into the activity for immediate feedback. Some examples include interactive activities like flash cards, quiz questions, matching, crossword puzzles, and others. Feedback will be discussed in further detail later in this chapter. Course announcements can be used to post general information. It is also important to notify students through an announcement if the educator is going to be unavailable.

Educator Interaction After Instruction

Educator interaction after instruction is typically in the form of feedback. Feedback is crucial to student success in online education (Bonnel, 2008). Educators can provide student feedback through a variety of methods. Educators can give student feedback through written electronic communication. With written feedback, the educator should be sure to clarify tone and use language that expresses the true intent of the communication (Bonnel, 2008; Weiss, 2000). Educators can also create audio files to provide students with detailed feedback (Mariana, 2001). Brookhart (2008) suggested educators can provide feedback through conversations with students. In the online environment, phone calls or audio chats provide modes of conversational feedback. In conversational feedback, the educator can ask the student questions (Brookhart, 2008) which can assist the educator in tailoring feedback to meet the student's specific needs. Feedback can also be provided to the individual student and/or groups of students (Bonnel, 2008; Vrasidas & McIssac, 2002). Educator feedback lets students know if their responses were correct and, if not, how to specifically correct their performance for future assignments. Educator feedback provides guidance (Berge, 2002), can increase student motivation (Berge, 2002; Hirumi, 2002), reinforces course concepts and content (Hirumi, 2002), and promotes learning (Koszalka & Ganesan, 2004).

Characteristics of Effective Feedback

1. Provide timely feedback throughout the learning process (Bonnel, 2008; Carr–Chellman & Duchastel, 2001; Chickering & Ehrmann; Caplan, 2005; Edwards, 2005; Hardy & Bower, 2004; Johnson & Aragon, 2003; Norton & Hathway, 2008; Sieber, 2005; Sitzman & Leners, 2006). Johnson and Aragon (2003) recommended that students receive grading feedback within one week of submitting the assignment.
2. Educators should clearly identify the information provided to students as feedback for a specific assignment or learning task (Bonnel, 2008).
3. Individual feedback should be personalized (Johnson & Aragon, 2003; Vrasidas & McIssac, 2002) and constructive (Bonnel, 2008; Hardy & Bower, 2005; Norton & Hathway, 2008; Sieber, 2005).
4. Cognitive or corrective feedback identifies areas that the student has achieved learning outcomes and areas that the student needs improvement (Johnson & Aragon, 2003; Martinez, 2004; Sieber, 2005). Feedback should begin with the positive aspects of student performance (Bonnel, 2008; Edwards, 2005). Brookhart (2008) indicated that positive feedback describes "...how the strengths in a student's work match the criteria for good work and how they show what the student is learning" (p. 57). The educator should address any improvements over previous work (Bonnel, 2008: Brookhart, 2008).
5. Feedback should include the specific grade with statements supporting the grade assigned (Edwards, 2005). The feedback should be specific and detailed (Brookhart, 2008; Sieber, 2005). The use of grading rubrics is very important in providing students with effective feedback. Educators can mark the level of the student's work on the rubric and supplement with more personalized and specific feedback. Provide tips or tasks the student can do to improve performance and promote success including examples (Brookhart, 2008; Edwards, 2005). The educator should reinforce expectations and remind students of available resources (Edwards, 2005).
6. Feedback should end with a statement(s) to motivate the student (Edwards, 2005). Martinez (2004), stated "motivational feedback encourages students to complete tasks, try harder, or achieve higher goals" (p. 268).

CHAPTER 6 APPLICATION EXERCISE

Use the same subject and module of instruction that you used for the Application Exercises for Chapters 3–5. Select four methods of content delivery, learning strategies, and teaching strategies to facilitate Student-Content Interaction for your module of instruction. Select four methods of Student-Student Interaction for your module of instruction. Complete the table below.

Subject:

Module of Instruction:

Method of Student-Content Interaction	Method of Student-Student Interaction

REFERENCES

Ally, M. (2004). Foundations of educational theory for online learning: In T. Anderson & F. Elloumi (Eds.), *Theory and practice of online learning* (pp. 3–31). Retrieved from http://cde.athabascauca/online_book/pdf/TPOL_chp01.pdf

Alonso, F., Lopez, G., Manrique, D., & Vines, J. M. (2008). Learning objects, learning objectives, and learning design. *Innovations in Education and Teaching International, 45*(4), 389–400.

Anderson, T. (2004). Teaching in an online learning context: In T. Anderson & F. Elloumi, *Theory and practice of online learning* (pp. 33–60). Retrieved from http://cde.athabascau.ca/online_book/pdf/TPOL_chp02.pdf.

Ascough, R. S. (2002). Designing for online education: Putting pedagogy before technology. *Teaching Theology and Religion, 5*(1), 17–29.

Azriel, J. A., Erthal, M. J., & Starr, E. (2005). Answers, questions and deceptions: What is the role of games in business education? *Journal of Education for Business, 81*(1), 9–13.

Baglione, S., & Nastanski, M. (2007). The superiority of online discussions: Faculty perceptions. *The Quarterly Review of Distance Education, 8*(2), 139–150.

Barab, S., Thomas, M., Dodge T., Carteaux, R., & Tuzon, H. (2005). Making learning fun: Quest atlantis, a game without guns. *Educational Technology Research and Development, 53*(1), 86–107.

Barbera, E. (2004). Quality in virtual education environments. *British Journal of Educational Technology, 35*(1), 13–20.

Beldarrain, Y. (2006). Distance education trends: Integrating new technologies to foster student interaction and collaboration. *Distance Education, 27*(2), 139–153.

Bennett, K., & McGee, P. (2005). Transformative power of the learning object debate. *Open Learning, 20*(1), 15–30.

Berge, Z. (2002). Active, interactive, and reflective learning. *The Quarterly Review of Distance Education, 3*(2), 181–190.

Bernstein, J. L., Scheerhorn, S., & Ritter, S. (2002). Using simulations and collaborative teaching to enhance introductory courses. *College Teaching, 50*(1), 9–12.

Beth, S., & Ayotte, M. (2006). Is there a place for games in the college classroom? *Teaching Professor, 20*(6), 3.

Bisoux, T. (2008). Teaching business in a web 2.0 world. *Biz2Ed, 7*(1), 28–35.

Black, P. (2006). Uses of blogs in legal education. *James Cook University Law Review, 13,* 8–29.

Blair, S., & Godsall, L. (2006). One school's experience in implementing eportfolios: Lessons learned. *The Quarterly Review of Distance Education, 7*(2), 145–154.

Bober, M. J., & Dennen, V. P. (2001). Intersubjectivity: Facilitating knowledge construction in online environments. *Education Media International, 38*(4), 241–250.

Bolin, A., Khramtsova, I., & Saarnio, D. (2005). Using student journals to stimulate authentic learning: Balancing Bloom's cognitive and affective domains. *Teaching of Psychology, 32*(3), 154–159.

Bonnel, W. (2008). Improving feedback to students in online courses. *Nursing Education Perspectives, 29*(5), 290–294.

Boud, D. (2001). Using journal writing to enhance reflective practice. *New Directions for Adult and Continuing Education, 90,* 9–17.

Boulos, M., & Wheeler, S. (2007). The emerging web 2.0 social software: An enabling suite of sociable technologies in health and health care education. *Health Information and Libraries Journal, 24,* 2–23.

Brookhart, S. (2008). Feedback that fits. *Educational Leadership, 65*(4), 54–59.

Buckley, W., & Smith, A. (2007). Application of multimedia technologies to enhance distance learning. *RE:View, 39*(2), 57–65.

Butcher, H., & Taylor, J. (2008). Using a wiki to enhance knowing participation in change in the teaching learning process. *Visions, 15(1),* 30–43.

Canada, M. (2002). Assessing e-folios in the online class. *New Directions for Teaching and Learning, 91,* 69–75.

Carraccio, C., & Englander, R. (2004). Evaluating competence using a portfolio: A literature review and web-based application to the ACGME competencies. *Teaching and Learning in Medicine, 16*(4), 381–387.

Caplan, D. (2004). The development of online courses. In T. Anderson & F. Elloumi (Eds.), *Theory and practice of online learning* (pp. 175–194). Retrieved from http://cde.athabascau.ca/online_book/pdf/TPOL_chp07.pdf

Carr–Chellman, A., & Duchastel, P. (2001). The ideal online course. *Library Trends, 50*(1), 145–158.

Challis, M. (1999). AMEE medical education guide no. 11(revised): Portfolio-based learning and assessment in medical education. *Medical Teacher, 21*(4), 370–386.

Challis, M. (2001). Portfolios and assessment: Meeting the challenge. *Medical Teacher, 3*(5), 437–440.

Chang, C. (2001). Construction and evaluation of a web-based learning portfolio system: An electronic assessment tool. *Innovations in Education and Teaching International, 38*(2), 144–155.

Chickering, A. W., & Ehrmann, S. C. (1996). Implementing the seven principles: Technology as a lever. *AAHE Bulletin, 49*(2), 3–6. Retrieved from http://aahea.org/bulletins/articles/sevenprinciples.htm.

Childress, M., & Braswell, R. (2006). Using massively multiplayer online role-playing games for online learning. *Distance Education, 27*(2), 187–196.

Chuang, H. (2008). Perspectives and issues of the creation for web-blog based electronic portfolios in teacher education. *British Journal of Educational Technology, 39*(1), 170–174.

Columbo, M., & Columbo, D. (2007). Blogging to improve instruction in differentiated science classrooms. *Phi Delta Kappan, 89*(1), 60–63.

Comer, S. (2005). Patient care simulations: Role playing to enhance clinical understanding. *Nursing Education Perspectives, 26*(6), 357–361.

Cook–Benjamin, L. (2001). Portfolio assessment: Benefits, issues of implementation, and reflections on its use. *Assessment Update, 13*(4), 6–7.

Corcoran, J., & Nicholson, C. (2004). Learning portfolios-evidence of learning: An examination of student perspectives. *Nursing In Critical Care, 9*(5), 230–237.

Cox, B., & Cox, B. (2008). Developing interpersonal and group dynamics through asynchronous threaded discussions: The use of discussion board in collaborative learning. *Education, 128*(4), 553–566.

Cox, B., Carr, T., & Hall, M. (2004). Evaluating the use of synchronous communication in two blended courses. *Journal of Computer Assisted Learning, 20*, 183–193.

Cuellar, N. (2002). The transition from classroom to online teaching. *Nursing Forum, 37*(3), 5–13.

Davis, A., & McGrail, E. (2009). The joy of blogging. *Educational Leadership, 66*(6), 74–77.

Davis, C., & Wilcock, E. (2005). Developing, implementing and evaluating case studies in material science. *European Journal of Engineering Education, 30*(1), 59–69.

Dearstyne. B. (2005). Blogs: The new information revolution? *The Information Management Journal, 39*(5), 38–44.

Delpier, T. (2006). Cases 101: Learning to teach with cases. *Nursing Education Perspectives, 27*(4), 204–209.

Driessen, E. W., Tartwijk, J. V., Overeem, K., Vermunt, J. D., & van der Vleuten, C. P. M.. (2005). Conditions for successful reflective use of portfolios in undergraduate medical education. *Medical Education, 39*, 1230–1235.

Ducate, L., & Lomicka, L. (2008). Adventures in the blogosphere: From blog readers to blog writers. *Computer Assisted Language Learning, 21*(1), 9–28.

Edgar, T. F. (2005). Lab courses go virtual. *Control Engineering, 52*(12), 22.

Edwards, T. (2005). Seven steps for providing constructive online discussion feedback successfully. *Online Classroom, 9*, 1, 6.

Elliot, M., Kaufmann, S., Gardner, R., & Burgess, G. (2002). Teaching conflict assessment and frame analysis though interactive web-based simulations. *The International Journal of Conflict Management, 13*(4), 320–340.

English, L. M., & Gillen, M. A. (2001). Journal writing in practice: From Vision to Reality. *New Directions for Adult and Continuing Education, 90*, 87–94.

Engstrom, M. & Jewett, D. (2005). Collaborative learning the wiki way. *TechTrends, 49*(6), 12– 15.

Ertmer, P., & Dillon, D. (1998). Shooting in the dark versus breaking it down: Understanding students' approaches to case-based instruction. *Qualitative Studies In Education, 11*(4), 605–622.

Fung, Y. (2004). Collaborative online learning: Interaction, patterns, and limiting factors. *Open Learning, 19*(2), 135–149.

Gaide, S. (2006). ePortfolios supercharge performance-based student assessment. *Distance Education Report, 10*(2), 4–6.

Gartland, M., & Field, T. (2004). Case method learning: Online exploration and collaboration for multicultural education. *Multicultural Perspectives 6*(1), 30–35.

Gibbs, H. J. (2004). Student portfolios: Documenting student success. *Techniques, 79*(5), 27–31.

Gillis, A. J. (2001). Journal writing in health education. *New Directions for Adult and Continuing Education, 90,* 49–58.

Glittenburg, C., & Binder, S. (2006). Using 3D computer simulations to enhance ophthalmic training. *Ophthalmic and Physiological Optics, 26,* 40–49.

Graham, C. (2002). Factors for effective learning groups in face-to-face and virtual environments. *The Quarterly Review of Distance Education, 3*(3), 307–319.

Gustafson, C. (2008). Blogging in the library. *Library Media Connection, 27*(3), 56–57.

Halat, E. (2008). A good teaching technique: WebQuests. *The Clearing House, 81*(3), 109–111.

Hampton, S. E., & Morrow, C. (2003). Reflective journaling and assessment. *Journal of Professional Issues in Engineering Education and Practice, 129*(4), 186–189.

Hardy, K. P., & Bower, B. L. (2004). Instructional and work life issues for distance learning faculty. *New Directions for Community Colleges, 128,* 47–54.

Hartley, D. (2006). Learning can be fun. *American Society for Training and Development, May,* 53–54.

Hasler–Waters, L., & Napier, W. (2002). Building and supporting team collaboration in the virtual classroom. *The Quarterly Review of Distance Education, 3*(3), 345–352.

Hawkes, W., & Coldeway, D. O. (2002). An analysis of team vs. faculty-based online course development: Implications for instructional design. *The Quarterly Review of Distance Education, 3*(4), 431–441.

Heimstra, R. (2001). Uses and benefits of journal writing. *New Directions for Adult and Continuing Education, 90,* 19–26.

Hewett, S. (2004). Electronic portfolios: Improving instructional practices. *TechTrends, 48*(5), 26–30.

Hines, R. A, & Pearl, C. E. (2004). Increasing interaction in web-based instruction: Using synchronous chats and asynchronous discussions. *Rural Special Education Quarterly, 23*(2), 33–36.

Hirumi, A. (2002). A framework for analyzing, designing, and sequencing planned elearning interactions. *The Quarterly Review of Distance Education, 3*(2), 141–160.

Horton, K., Davenport, E., Hall, H., & Rosenbaum, H. (2002). Internet simulations for teaching, learning, and research: An investigation of e-commerce interactions and practice in the virtual economy. *Education for Information, 20,* 237–252.

Huang, H. (2002). Toward constructivism for adult learners in online learning environments. *British Journal of Educational Technology, 33*(1), 27–37.

Hubbs, D. L., & Brand, C. F. (2005). The paper mirror: Understanding reflective journaling. *Journal of Experiential Education, 28*(1), 60–71.

Im, Y., & Lee, O. (2003). Pedagogical implications of online discussion for pre-service teacher training. *Journal of Research on Technology in Education, 36*(2), 155–170.

Iwasiw, C., & Goldenberg, D. (1993). Peer teaching among nursing students in the clinical area: Effects on student learning. *Journal of Advanced Nursing, 18,* 659–668.

Jarvis, P. (2001). Journal writing in higher education. *New Directions for Adult and Continuing Education, 90,* 79–86.

Jeffries, P. (2005). A framework for designing, implementing, and evaluating simulations used as teaching strategies in nursing. *Nursing Education Perspectives, 26*(2), 96–103.

Johnson, S. D., & Aragon, S. R. (2003). An instructional strategy framework for online learning environments. *New Directions for Adult and Continuing Education, 100,* 31–43.

Kneebone, R. (2003). Simulation in surgical training: Educational issues and practical implications. *Medical Education, 32,* 267–277.

Kneebone, R., & ApSimon D. (2001). Surgical skills training: Simulation and multimedia combined. *Medical Education, 35,* 909–915.

Knoble, M., & Lankshear, C. (2009). Wikis, digital literacies, and professional growth. *Journal of Adolescent and Adult Literacy, 52*(7), 631–634.

Koszalka, T. A., & Ganesan, R. (2004). Designing online courses: A taxonomy to guide strategic use of features available in course management systems (CMS) in distance education. *Distance Education, 25*(2), 243–256.

Kunselman, J., & Johnson, K. (2004). Using the case method to facilitate learning. *College Teaching, 52*(3), 87–92.

Lebaron, J., & Miller, D. (2005). The potential of jigsaw role playing to promote the social construction of knowledge in an online graduate education course. *Teachers College Record, 107*(8), 1654–1674.

Li, Q. (2004). Knowledge building community: Keys for using online forums. *TechTrends 48*(4), 24–28.

Lin, S., & Overbaugh, R. (2007). The effect of student choice of online discussion format on tiered achievement and student satisfaction. *Journal of Research on Technology in Education, 39*(4), 399–415.

Malasky, E. (1984). Instructional strategies: Nonmedia. In L. Nadler (Ed.), *Handbook of human resource development* (pp. 9.2–9.30). New York: John Wiley and Sons.

Mariana, M. (2001). Distance learning in postsecondary education: Learning whenever, wherever. *Occupational Outlook Quarterly, 45*(2), 2–9.

Marsick, V. (1990). Case Study. In M. Galbraith (Ed.), *Adult learning methods: A guide for effective instruction* (pp. 225–246). Malabar, Florida: Robert F. Kreiger Publishing.

Martinez, R. (2004). Online education: Designing for the future in appraiser education. *Appraiser Journal, 72*(3), 266–273.

Mason, R. (2006). Learning technologies for adult continuing education. *Studies in Continuing Education, 28*(2), 121–133.

Mason, R., Pegler, C., & Weller, M. (2004). E-portfolios: An assessment tool for online courses. *British Journal of Educational Technology, 35*(6), 717–727.

Mayer, R. W., & Moreno, R. (2002). Animation as an aid to multimedia learning. *Educational Psychology Review, 14*(1), 87–99.

Mayo, J. (2004). Using case-based instruction to bridge the gap between theory and practice in psychology of adjustment. *Journal of Constructivist Psychology, 17,* 137–146.

McCarthy, J., & Anderson, L. (2000). Active learning techniques versus traditional teaching styles: Two experiments from history and political science. *Innovative Higher Education, 24*(4), 279–294.

McConnell, D. (2005). Examining the dynamics of networked e-learning groups and communities. *Studies in Higher Education, 30*(1), 25–42.

McKeachie, W., & Svinicki, M. (2006). *McKeachie's teaching tips: Strategies, research, and theory for college and university teachers.* Boston, MA: Houghton Mifflin Company.

McLoughlin, D., & Mynard, J. (2009). An analysis of higher order thinking in online discussions. *Innovations in Education and Teaching International, 46*(2), 147–160.

Mercado, S. (2000). Pre-managerial business education: A role for role-plays? *Journal of Further and Higher Education, 24*(1), 117–126.

Merrill, M., & Gilbert, C. (2008). Effective peer interaction in a problem-centered instructional strategy. *Distance Education, 29*(2), 199–207.

Mitchell, R. C. (2004). Combining cases and computer simulations in strategic management courses. *Journal of Education for Business, 79*(4), 198–204.

Minocha, S., & Thomas, P. (2007). Collaborative learning in a wiki environment: Experiences from a software engineering course. *New Review of Hypermedia and Multimedia, 13*(2), 187–209.

Morgan, B., & Smith, R. (2008). A wiki for classroom writing. *The Reading Teacher, 62*(1), 80–82.

Nakerud, S., & Scaletta, K. (2008). Blogging in the academy. *New Directions for Student Services, 124,* 71–87.

Nieymer, E. (1995). The case for case studies. *Training and Development, 49*(1), 50–52.

Northrup, P. T. (2002). Online learners' preferences for interaction. *The Quarterly Review of Distance Education, 3*(2), 219–226.

Norton, P., & Hathaway, D. (2008). Exploring two teacher education online designs: A classroom of one or many? *Journal of Research on Technology in Education, 40*(4), 475–495.

Orland–Barak, L. (2005). Portfolio's as evidence of reflective practice: What remains 'untold'. *Educational Research, 47*(1), 25–44.

Parr, G., Wilson, J., Godinho, S., & Longaretti, L. (2004). Improving pre-service teacher learning through peer teaching: Process, people, and product. *Mentoring and Tutoring, 12*(2), 187–203.

Paulus, T. (2005). Collaborative and cooperative approaches to online group work: The impact of task type. *Distance Education, 26*(1), 111–125.

Pivec, M., & Dziabenko, O. (2004). Game-based learning in universities and lifelong learning : "Unigame: Social skills and knowledge training" game concept. *Journal of Universal Computer Science, 10*(1), 14–25.

Pitts, J., Coles, C., & Thomas, P. (2001). Enhancing reliability in portfolio assessment: 'shaping' the portfolio. *Medical Teacher, 23*(4), 351–356.

Richardson, W. (2006). The educator's guide to the read/write web. *Educational Leadership, 63*(4), 24–27.

Riley, W., & Anderson, P. (2006). Randomized study on the impact of cooperative learning distance education in public health. *The Quarterly Review of Distance Education, 7*(2), 129–144.

Robbins, J. (2006). Electronic portfolios as a bridge. *Intervention in School and Clinic, 42*(2), 107–113.

Roy, M. J., Sticha, D. L., Kraus, P. L., & Olsen, D. E. (2006). Simulation and virtual reality in medical education and therapy: A protocol. *CyberPsychology and Behavior, 9*(2), 245–247.

Ruiz, J. G., Mintzer, M. J., & Issenberg, S.B. (2006). Learning objects in medical education. *Medical Teacher, 28*(7), 599–605.

Sandars, J. (2005). Using webquests to enhance worked based learning. *Worked Based Learning in Primary Care, 3*, 210–217.

Sanders, J. (2007). The potential of blogs and wikis in healthcare education. *Education for Primary Care, 18*, 16–21

Schwartzman, R. (2006). Virtual group problem solving in the basic communication course: Lessons for online learning. *Journal of Instructional Psychology, 33*(1), 3–14.

Sheehy, G. (2008). The wiki as knowledge repository: Using a wiki in a community of practice to strengthen K–12 education. *TechTrends, 56*(6), 55–60.

Shepard, G., & Jensen, G. M. (2002). *Handbook of teaching for physical therapists.* Woburn, MA: Butterworth-Heinemann.

Shi, M., Bonk, C. J., & Magjuka, R. J. (2006). Time management strategies for online education. *International Journal of Instructional Technology and Distance Learning, 3*(2). Retrieved from http://itdl.org/Journal/Feb_06/article01.htm.

Shim, B., Brock, D., & Jenkins, L. (2005). Developing practical criteria for evaluating online patient simulations: A preliminary study. *Medical Teacher, 27*(2), 175–177.

Sieber, J. C. (2005). Misconceptions and realities about teaching online. *Science and Engineering Ethics, 11*, 329–340.

Sims, R., Dobbs, G., & Hand, T. (2002). Enhancing quality in online learning: Scaffolding, , and design through proactive evaluation. *Distance Education, 23*(2), 135–148.

Sitzman, K., & Leners, D. (2006). Student perceptions of caring in online baccalaureate education. *Nursing Education Perspectives, 27*(5), 254–259.

Skiba, D. (2005). Do your students wiki? *Nursing Education Perspectives, 26*(2), 120–121.

Smith, J. C., & Diaz, R. (2002). *Evolving uses of technology in cased based teacher education*. Retrieved from http://www.literacy.org/products/SmithDiazSITE2002. pdf

Smith, K. (1999). *Characteristics of an effective case study*. Retrieved from http://www. nscc.edu/seatec/pages_resources/forum_papers_pdf/smith.pdf

Smith, K., & Tillema, H. (2003). Clarifying different types of portfolio use. *Assessment & Evaluation in Higher Education, 28*(6), 625–648.

Snadden, D., & Thomas, M. (1998). The use of portfolio learning in medical education. *Medical Teacher, 20*(3), 192–199.

Sturgeon, J. (2008). Five don'ts of classroom blogging. *THE Journal, 35(2),* 26–30.

Tang, T., Hernandez, E., & Adams, S. (2004). Learning by teaching: A peer-teaching model for diversity training in medical school. *Teaching and Learning in Medicine, 16*(1), 60–63.

Thompson, L., & Ku, H. (2006). A case study of online collaborative learning. *The Quarterly Review of Distance Education, 7*(4), 361–375.

Tu, C., & Corry, M. (2002). ELearning communities. *The Quarterly Review of Distance Education, 3*(2), 207–218.

Tutty, J., & Klein, J. (2008). Computer-mediated instruction: a comparison of online and face-to-face instruction. *Educational Technology Research and Development, 56,* 101–124.

Venezky, R. L., & Oney, B. A. (2004). *Creating and using portfolios on the alphabet superhighway*. Retrieved from http://www.ash.udel.edu/ash/teacher/portfolio. html

Vernon, T., & Peckham, D. (2002). The benefits of 3D modeling and animation in medical education. *Journal of Audiovisual Media in Medicine, 25*(4), 142–148.

Vrasidas, C., & McIsaac, M. S. (2002). Principles of pedagogy and evaluation for web-based learning. *Educational Media International, 37*(2), 105–111.

Wang, C. H. (2005). Questioning skills facilitate online synchronous discussions. *Journal of Computer Assisted Learning, 21,* 303–313.

Wang, S., & Hsua, H. (2008). Reflections on using blogs to expand in-class discussion. *TechTrends, 52*(3), 81–85.

Wanstreet, C. (2006). Interaction in online environments: A review of the literature. *Review of Distance Education, 7*(4), 399–411.

Weiss, R. (2000). Humanizing the online classroom. *New Directions for Teaching and Learning, 84,* 47–51.

Wentland, D. (2004). A guide for determining which teaching methodology to utilize in economic education: Trying to improve how economic education is communicated to students. *Education, 124*(4), 640–648.

West, R. Wright, G., Gabbitas, B., & Graham, C. (2006). Reflections from the introduction of blogs and RSS feeds into a preservice instructional technology course. *Tech Trends, 50*(4), 54–60.

Wheeler, S., Yeomans, P., & Wheeler, D. (2008). The good, the bad, and the wiki: Evaluating student generated content for collaborative learning. *British Journal of Educational Technology, 39*(6), 987–995.

White, C. P. (2004). Student portfolios: An alternative way of encouraging and evaluating student learning. *New Directions for Teaching and Learning, 100,* 37–42.

Whitsed, N. (2005). Learning and teaching. *Health Information and Libraries Journal, 22,* 74–77.

Wickersham, L. E., & Chambers, S. M. (2006). ePortfolios: Using technology to assess and enhance student learning. *Education, 126*(4), 738–746.

Williams, S. (1992). Putting case-based instruction into context: Examples from legal and medical education. *The Journal of The Learning Sciences, 2*(4), 367–427.

Wright, S. (1996). Case-based instruction: Linking theory to practice. *Physical Educator, 53*(4), 190.

Yoon, W. (2003). In search of meaningful online learning experiences. *New Directions for Adult and Continuing Education, 100,* 19–30.

CHAPTER 7

ASSESSMENT AND GRADING RUBRICS

This chapter will:

1. Identify important factors in regards to online assessment.
2. Identify best practices for creating online tests/exams.
3. Define self-assessment.
4. Identify important factors in regards to self-assessment.
5. Identify advantages for using self-assessment.
6. Identify disadvantages for using self-assessment.
7. Discuss strategies for course implementation of self-assessment.
8. Define peer assessment.
9. Identify important factors in regards to peer assessment.
10. Identify advantages for using peer assessment.
11. Identify disadvantages for using peer assessment.
12. Discuss strategies for course implementation of peer assessment.
13. Identify the purposes, uses, and advantages of grading rubrics.
14. Identify strategies for course implementation of grading rubrics.

A Learner Centered Approach To Online Education, pages 117–131.
Copyright © 2013 by Information Age Publishing
117

The final step in online course development and design is to choose assessment methods. According to Gaytan and McEwen (2007), "the main purposes of assessment are to monitor student learning, improve academic programs, and enhance teaching and learning" (p. 118). Assessment methods should be aligned with learning outcomes and instructional objectives. Subjective assessment methods should have corresponding grading rubrics. Students should also receive feedback for subjective assessment methods. Please refer to Student-Instructor Interaction in Chapter 6 for more information on feedback. This chapter includes information on assessment including online tests/exams, self-assessment, and peer assessment. This chapter also includes information on grading rubrics.

ASSESSMENT

Assessment is a means of measuring progress (Adams & King, 1995); obtainment of skills and knowledge (Davies, 2006); and obtainment of course and program learning outcomes. Liu & Carless (2006) indicated that "... there are two main purposes of assessment: a certification (or summative) purpose and a learning (or formative purpose)" (p. 279). A variety of assessment methods or strategies should be included in an online course (Gaytan & McEwen, 2007).

Learning and teaching strategies such as projects; portfolios; journals; papers; presentations; discussion questions; peer teaching; case studies; professional development plans; as well as others, can also be used as assessment methods. Please refer to Student-Content Interaction in Chapter 6 for more information on these learning and teaching strategies. Assessment methods also include online tests/exams, self-assessment, and peer assessment.

Online Tests/Exams

Online tests/exams can have the following question types: true/false, fill in the blank, matching, multiple choice, short answer, and essay. The type of question used should be based on the learning outcomes and instructional objectives. Short answer and essay questions are open-ended question types (Schuwirth & Van Der Vleuten, 2004). A short answer question typically requires a student to reproduce information. An essay question typically requires a student to process information (Schuwirth & Van Der Vleuten, 2004). See the following best practices for creating online tests/exams:

1.   Creating question pools within the course management system will allow the educator to quickly change tests/exams within the course by selecting different questions. This also allows the educator to

allow random questions on the test/exam based on degree of difficulty.

2. To facilitate academic integrity for online tests/exams, tests/exams can be set up to shuffle questions and to shuffle answers within questions. If setting up questions to shuffle answers within questions there should be no questions that have a choice of "all of the above" or that choose more than one choice. Also, in regards to academic integrity, tests should be timed. Educators can require that students use software that does not allow other applications to be opened during a test/exam. It may also be appropriate to have tests/exams proctored.

3. The course management system may also allow the educator to determine if a student receives immediate feedback or feedback after the test/exam is closed. The educator can also determine what type of feedback the student receives including: student responses, correct answers, score, and more.

Self-Assessment

Self-assessment is important for learning course content and for lifelong learning (Lew, Alwis, & Schmidt, 2010; Taras, 2010). Self-assessment requires learners to use specific standards to assess their own work and determine if the work meets those standards (Andrade & Du, 2007; Andrade & Valtcheva, 2009; De Wever, Van Keer, Schellens, & Valcke, 2009; Sargeant, Mann, Van der Vleuten, & Metsemakers, 2008). Students then revise the work as needed prior to submission for grading (Andrade & Du, 2007; Andrade & Valtcheva, 2009).

Advantages
There are numerous advantages for using self-assessment:

- Self-assessment increases opportunities for student-content interaction.
- Self-assessment can lead to increased learning; improved assessment scores (Andrade & Du, 2007; Lew et al., 2010); and a better understanding of the assessment process (Hanrahan & Isaacs, 2001; Taras; 2010).
- Self assessment promotes critical thinking skills (Adeyemi, 2012; Amo & Jareño, 2011; De Wever et al., 2009; Hanrahan & Isaacs, 2001; Macdonald, 2001; Sargeant et al., 2008).
- Self-assessment increases learning quality and improves work quality (Adams & King, 1995; Andrade & Du, 2007).

- Self-assessment promotes active learning and helps students identify strengths and weaknesses (Andrade & Du, 2007; Andrade &
Valtcheva, 2009; Adeyemi, 2012; Hanrahan & Isaacs, 2001; Lew et al.,
2010; Macdonald, 2001; Sargeant et al., 2008; Taras, 2010).
- Self-assessment promotes self-efficacy, autonomy, responsibility, and
accountability (Adeyemi, 2012; Adams & King, 1995; De Wever et al.,
2009; Lew et al., 2010).
- Self- assessment promotes reflection (Adeyemi, 2012; Amo & Jare-
ño, 2011; De Wever et al., 2009; Lew et al., 2010; Macdonald, 2001;
Sargeant et al., 2008; Taras, 2010).
- Self-assessment increases motivation (Adeyemi, 2012; Amo & Jareño,
2011; Andrade & Du, 2007).
- Students can use self-assessment to check work and revise as needed
(Andrade & Du, 2007) prior to submission for grading.
- Self-assessment can assist the educator with evaluation (Adams &
King, 1995; Taras, 2010).
- Self-assessment promotes lifelong learning (Lew et al., 2010; Taras,
2010).

Disadvantages

There are some disadvantages for using self-assessment.

- Students may not see the value in self-assessment (Lew et al., 2010).
- Students may feel the process is too time-consuming.
- Students may not accept the responsibility of self-assessment and may
feel assessment is the responsibility of the educator (Adams & King,
1995; Amo & Jareño, 2011).
- Students may be unclear on expectations and criteria (Adams &
King, 1995).
- Student ratings may be not accurate (Hanrahan & Isaacs, 2001; Lew
et al., 2010). Students may rate themselves too high (Adams & King,
1995; Amo & Jareño, 2011; Sargeant et al., 2008) or too low (Adams & King, 1995). This can lead to issues with reliability and validity
(Lew et al., 2010; Sargeant et al., 2008).

Strategies for Course Implementation

1. Self-assessment should be treated as a learning activity (Liu &
Carless, 2006). Self-assessment should be formative in nature and
should not be counted toward a grade (Andrade & Valtcheva, 2009;
Andrade & Du 2007).

2. Self- assessment should be educator facilitated (Sargeant et al., 2008).
3. Provide rationale for the self-assessment activity (Andrade & Valtcheva, 2009).
4. Clarify expectations and criteria for the self-assessment assignment using a marking sheet, checklist, or grading rubric (Adams & King, 1995; Andrade & Du, 2007; Andrade & Valtcheva, 2009; Andrade, Wang, Du, & Akawi, 2009; Hanrahan & Isaacs, 2001; Sargeant et al., 2008).
5. Provide guidelines and instruction on applying assessment criteria (Adams & King, 1995; Andrade & Du, 2007; Andrade & Valtcheva, 2009; Hanrahan & Isaacs, 2001).
6. Provide examples of work that is at various levels (Adams & King, 1995; Andrade & Valtcheva, 2009; Andrade et al., 2009; Taras, 2010).
7. Provide opportunities for practice (Adams & King, 1995; Hanrahan & Isaacs, 2001).
8. Provide feedback to students regarding self-assessment (Andrade & Du, 2007; Andrade & Valtcheva, 2009; Sargeant et al., 2009).
9. Provide a revision period after self-assessment (Andrade & Valtcheva, 2009) for students to revise their work prior to submission for grading (Andrade & Du, 2007).

Peer-Assessment

Peer assessment is a process in which a student assesses the work of another student or group of students and gives feedback (Al–Barakat & Al–Hassan, 2009; Ballantyne, Hughes, & Mylonas, 2002; Henning & Marty, 2008; Liu & Carless, 2006; Van den Berg, Admiraal, & Pilot, 2006; Vickerman, 2009; Vu & Dall'Alba, 2007). The focus of peer assessment should be on feedback (Falchikov & Goldfinch, 2000; Liu & Carless, 2006; Topping, 2009). Due to the controversy surrounding the assigning of grades by peers (Vu & Dall'Alba, 2007), this practice is not recommended. Peer assessment can be used for both assessment and learning purposes (Chen & Tsai, 2009; Tamjid & Birjandi, 2011; Wen & Tsai, 2006).

Advantages

There are numerous advantages for using peer assessment:

*   Peer assessment increases opportunities for student-student and student-content interaction.
*   Peer assessment improves self-assessment, self-awareness, and observation skills; promotes student learning; and increases student understanding of the assessment process (Adeyemi, 2012; Al–Barakat &

Al–Hassan, 2009; Amo & Jareño, 2011; Ballantyne et al., 2002; Bloxham & West, 2004; Cestone, Levine, & Lane, 2008; Davis, Kumtepe, & Aydeniz, 2007; Hanrahan & Isaacs, 2001; Henning & Marty, 2008; Langan, Shuker, Cullen, Penny, Preziosi, & Wheater, 2008; Liu & Carless, 2006; Pharo, & De Salas, 2009: Macdonald, 2001; Tamjid & Birjandi, 2011; Wen & Tsai, 2006; Vickerman, 2009; Vu & Dall'Alba, 2007).

- Peer assessment promotes critical thinking skills (Amo & Jareño, 2011; Ballantyne et al., 2002; Bloxham & West, 2004; Cestone, Levine, & Lane, 2008; Chen and Tsai, 2009; Davis et al., 2007; Hanrahan & Isaacs, 2001; Hou, Chang, & Sung, 2007; Joordens, Desa, & Pare, 2009; Macdonald, 2001; Pharo, & de Salas, 2009; Sivan, 2000; Willey & Gardner, 2010).
- Peer assessment can improve learning quality (Bouzidi & Jalliet, 2009; Cestone, Levine, & Lane, 2008; Topping, 2009; Wen & Tsai, 2006).
- Peer assessment promotes active learning (Ballantyne et al., 2002; Langan et al., 2008; Wen & Tsai, 2006).
- Peer assessment promotes self efficacy, autonomy, and responsibility (Adeyemi, 2012; Al–Barakat & Al–Hassan, 2009; Amo & Jareño, 2011; Ballantyne et al., 2002; Bouzidi & Jalliet, 2009; Davis et al., 2007; Langan et al., 2008; Pharo, & De Salas, 2009; Macdonald, 2001; Sivan, 2000; Tamjid & Birjandi, 2011; Wen & Tsai, 2006; Vickerman, 2009).
- Peer assessment enhances reflection (Austi et al., 2008; Langan et al., 2008; Macdonald, 2001; Sivan, 2000; Topping, 2009; Willey & Gardner, 2010).
- Peer assessment promotes interpersonal skills (Ballantyne et al., 2002; Cestone et al., 2008; Davis et al, 2007; Hanrahan & Isaacs, 2001; Tamjid & Birjandi, 2011); increases motivation (Al–Barakat & Al–Hassan, 2009; Henning & Marty, 2008); and increases student confidence (Al–Barakat & Al–Hassan, 2009; Ballantyne et al., 2002; Bloxham & West, 2004; Cestone et al., 2008; Pharo, & De Salas, 2009; Poon, McNaught, Lam, & Kwan, 2009; Sivan, 2000).
- Peer assessment improves the ability to "...give and receive criticism" (Ballantyne et al., 2002, p. 429).
- Peer assessment helps to ensure fairness in team assignments (Cestone et al., 2008; Willey & Gardner, 2010).
- Peer assessment provides more opportunities for feedback and an increase in frequency for feedback (Ballantyne et al., 2002; Sitthiworachart & Joy, 2008; Topping, 2009; Vickerman, 2009; Willey & Gardner, 2010).
- Peer assessment can aid in educator assessment (Chen & Tsai, 2009).
- Peer assessment can be used at all levels (Falchikov & Goldfinch, 2000). However, using peer assessment with higher level students

may result in increased student satisfaction with the peer assessment process (Ballantyne et al., 2002).

- Peer assessment promotes lifelong learning (Ballantyne et al., 2002; Hanrahan & Isaacs, 2001; Willey & Gardner, 2010).

Disadvantages

There are some disadvantages for using peer assessment.

- There may be resistance to peer assessment as students may feel peer assessment is the responsibility of the educator and may not accept the responsibility to evaluate peers (Amo & Jareño, 2011; Ballantyne et al., 2002; Cestone et al., 2008; Chen & Tsai, 2009; Liu & Carless, 2006; Wen & Tsai, 2006).
- Some students may not be able to recognize deficiencies (Bloxham & West, 2004), may interpret criteria incorrectly (Macdonald, 2001; Vu & Dall'Alba, 2007), and may not be comfortable in assessing the work of other students and providing feedback (Ballantyne et al., 2002; Hanrahan & Isaacs, 2001; Lin & Carless, 2006; Wen & Tsai, 2006; Vickerman, 2009; Vu & Dall'Alba, 2007).
- Students may be uncomfortable with other students viewing their work and may feel that peers are not qualified or capable of assessing their work (Al–Barakat & Al–Hassan, 2009; Ballantyne et al., 2002; Cartney, 2010; Davis et al, 2007; Lin & Carless, 2006; Poon et al., 2009; Sitthiworachart & Joy, 2008; Wen & Tsai, 2006; Vu & Dall'Alba, 2007).
- Peer assessment may be biased if students know each other or develop relationships (Al–Barakat & Al–Hassan, 2009; Bouzidi & Jalliet, 2009; Ballantyne et al., 2002; Chen & Tsai, 2009; Falchikov & Goldfinch, 2000; Vu & Dall'Alba, 2007) which among other issues can lead to reliability and validity issues (Falchikov & Goldfinch, 2000; Hanrahan & Isaacs, 2001; Langan, Shuker, Cullen, Penny, Preziosi, & Wheater, 2008; Liu & Carless, 2006; Topping, 2009; Wen & Tsai, 2006).
- Students may feel the peer assessment process is too time consuming (Ballantyne et al., 2002; Hanrahan & Isaacs, 2001; Lin & Carless, 2006; Macdonald, 2001; Vu & Dall'Alba, 2007).
- Peer assessment can be time consuming for educators to develop and implement (Ballantyne et al., 2002; Vu & Dall'Alba, 2007).

Strategies for Course Implementation

1. Treat peer assessment as a learning activity (Adeyemi, 2012; Liu & Carless, 2006; Sitthiworachart & Joy, 2008; Willey & Gardner, 2010).

2. Provide rationale for the peer assessment activity (Vu & Dall'Alba, 2007).
3. Clarify criteria for the peer assessment assignment, providing guidelines and instruction on assessment (including providing and receiving constructive feedback), as well as assessment criteria (Ballantyne et al., 2002; Chen & Tsai, 2009; Davis et al., 2007; Hanrahan & Isaacs, 2001; Macdonald, 2001; Pharo & de Salas, 2009; Poon et al., 2009; Sivan, 2000; Topping, 2009; Vu & Dall'Alba, 2007; Wen & Tsai, 2006).
4. Use marking sheets, checklists, (Cartney, 2010; Hanrahan & Isaacs, 2001; Pharo, & de Salas, 2009) or grading rubrics with emphasis on peer feedback (Liu & Carless, 2006; McMahon, 2010; Vu & Dall'Alba, 2007).
5. Provide examples of work that is at various levels (Hanrahan & Isaacs, 2001; Topping, 2009).
6. Provide practice sessions for peer assessment (Ballantyne et al., 2002; Hanrahan & Isaacs, 2001; Topping, 2009).
7. Randomly assign peer assessors (Chen & Tsai, 2009). It is recommended to have more than one assessor (Bouzidi & Jalliet, 2009; Davis et al., 2007; Liu & Carless, 2006; Vickerman, 2009) but not to have large groups of students in a peer assessor group (Falchikov & Goldfinch, 2000). Topping (2009) recommended to "...aim for same-ability peer matching" (p. 25). Anonymous assignment of peer assessors may lead to more honest, valid, and reliable feedback (Ballantyne et al., 2002; Hanrahan & Isaacs, 2001; Wen & Tsai, 2006; Vickerman, 2009).
8. The educator should facilitate, moderate, and guide the process (Bouzidi & Jalliet, 2009; Hou, Chang, & Sung, 2007; Topping, 2009).
9. Evaluate and check the quality of peer assessment by comparing the assessment with other peer's assessment and the educator's assessment (Topping, 2009), especially with the initial peer assessment activity. Provide feedback to student assessors regarding the peer assessment (Topping, 2009).
10. Award points for the assessment of a peer or peers (Ballantyne et al., 2002; Davies, 2006; Liu & Carless, 2006). Ballantyne et al. (2002), recommended 10–15% of the total score for the assignment.

GRADING RUBRICS

Rubrics provide students with a list of evaluative criteria, levels of quality with quality definitions, and a scoring strategy for specific assignments or assessments (Andrade, 2000; Popham, 1997). A rubric should be used as an instructional tool and can be created by the educator or co-created with students (Andrade, 2005). Students should be given a rubric along with the particular assignment/assessment instructions. The rubric is important to help students identify the gradable components of the assignment/assessment and how each component will be graded (Stefl–Mabry, 2004). The rubric can be used by the student as a working guide as the student completes the assignment/assessment (Jackson & Larkin, 2002; Leonhardt, 2005). Students can also use the rubric for self-assessment or peer assessment prior to submitting their final assignment/assessment (Andrade, 2005). By using the rubric as a working guide for assignment/assessment completion and a tool for peer and/or self assessment, the rubric provides a means of formative assessment (Jackson & Larkin, 2002).

Educators use rubrics to "assess process, performance, and progress" (Whitaker, Salend, & Duhaney, 2001, p. 9). A rubric allows the educator to provide very specific feedback about the quality of student work, thus providing opportunities for the student to learn and improve performance (Andrade, 2005). The rubric also serves as a scoring guide for the educator (Leonhardt, 2005) as the educator assigns grades (Andrade, 2005), thus providing summative assessment as the total learning process is evaluated (Jackson & Larkin, 2002).

Advantages

There are numerous advantages for using rubrics.

- A rubric helps students understand the expectations of an assignment/assessment prior to beginning the assignment/assessment (Jackson & Larkin, 2002; Whitaker et al., 2001). This helps the student focus on the specific criteria of the assignment/assessment (Andrade, 2005). Whitaker et al. (2001) indicated that rubrics help students develop critical thinking skills.
- Students are able to self assess their work (Whitaker et al., 2001), thus allowing the student to monitor their progress and "become aware of the quality of work through judging their own performance and their peer's assignments against the standards set in the rubric" (Jackson & Larkin, 2002, p. 41).
- A common advantage provided to students through the use of rubrics is the provision of feedback. Students can also use the rubric as a check list prior to submitting the final assignment/assessment (Jackson & Larkin, 2002). The feedback received from self-assessment, peer assessment, and educator assessment can improve learning and performance (Andrade, 2005; Stefl–Mabry, 2004).

- Andrade et al. (2007) suggested that "...rubric use can be related to improvements in the quality of students' writing and knowledge of the qualities of effective writing" (p. 287).
- Rubrics help educators orient toward objectives and focus instruction toward those objectives (Andrade, 2005).
- A rubric allows the educator to clearly indicate assignment/assessment objectives and expectations (Andrade, 2000; Stefl–Mabry, 2004).
- Rubrics also allow easier grading and a less time consuming method of providing feedback (Lewis, Berghoff, & Pheeny, 1999).
- Rubrics also assist the educator in fair and unbiased grading (Andrade, 2005).

Strategies for Course Implementation

1. Develop the assignment.
2. Determine the point value for the assignment.
3. Determine the scoring strategy. A scoring strategy is an important component of a rubric. Rubrics can use a holistic or analytic scoring strategy (Popham, 1997; Whitaker et al., 2001). The holistic scoring strategy is used when evaluative criteria are difficult to separate and the assignment/assessment is assigned a single score or rating describing the overall assignment/assessment (Jackson & Larkin, 2002; Popham, 1997; Whitaker et al., 2001). The analytic scoring strategy is used to give individual evaluative criteria scores (Whitaker et al., 2001). Due to the process oriented nature of analytic rubrics (Jackson & Larkin, 2002), these rubrics can be used to provide specific feedback to students to support learning (Whitaker et al., 2001). Using the analytic scoring strategy each of the scores for the evaluative criterion may or may not be aggregated into a single overall score (Popham, 1997).
4. Identify evaluative criteria for the assignment and determine the point value for each level of the evaluative criteria. Evaluative criteria are the specific components that will be evaluated and are different from rubric to rubric depending on the specific assignment/assessment (Popham, 1997). It is recommended to have three to five evaluative components in a grading rubric (Leonhardt, 2005; Popham, 1997) which can be weighted differently or

have equal weights (Popham, 1997). The evaluative criteria can be determined by the educator alone or from student input.

5. Once the evaluative criteria have been identified, quality definitions are used to "describe the way qualitative differences to student's responses are to be judged" (Popham, 1997, p. 72) for each qualitative level and a corresponding score is assigned to each qualitative level. The qualitative levels range from the highest proficiency level to the lowest proficiency level (Leonhardt, 2005).

6. Design the scoring grid and include quality definitions for each level of proficiency for each of the evaluative criteria. Ensure that the manner in which each level of proficiency is scored is clearly identified (Stefl–Mabry, 2004). Determine the value that will be assigned to each level of proficiency.

7. Post the assignment, rubric, and provide instructions on how to use the rubric.

8. Encourage students to use the rubric for self-assessment and/or peer assessment prior to submitting the final assignment.

9. Use the rubric to evaluate assignments (Whitaker et al., 2001).

10. Evaluate the rubric (Whitaker et al., 2001).

11. Revise the rubric as needed (Jackson & Larkin, 2002).

Sample Rubric

Below is an example of a rubric for a writing assignment with graded elements of knowledge and critical thinking, grammar/spelling, and length.

Item	5	4	3	2	1	0
Knowledge and Critical Thinking	Accurate answer with connections made between course readings	Accurate answer but no connections with course readings	Incomplete answer	Inaccurate information	Off Subject	Absent content
Grammar and Spelling	No errors	1 error	2 errors	3 errors	4 errors	5 or more errors
Length	5 paragraphs	4 paragraphs	3 paragraphs	2 paragraphs	1 paragraph	Less than 1 paragraph

Resources for Rubrics

Rubistar®	Rubistar® is a free web-based tool for creating rubrics. http://rubistar.4teachers.org/index.php
Kathy Schrock's Guide for Educators®	Kathy Schrock's Guide for Educators® includes assessment and rubric information. http://school.discovery.com/schrockguide/assess.html
ThinkingGear®	ThinkingGear® provides information on creating and using rubrics. http://www.thinkinggear.com/tools/rubrics.cfm

CONCLUSION

Online Test/Exams can have a variety of question types. When designing online test/exams, the educator should set options to facilitate academic integrity. The educator can chose the type of feedback and when the student receives the feedback for online tests/exams.

Self-assessment and peer assessment are important assessment measures to include in an online course with numerous documented advantages. Feedback is an important element for both self-assessment and peer assessment. Self-assessment requires students to assess their own work and then revise prior to submission for grading. Peer assessment requires students to evaluate the work of another student or student and provide feedback.

The use of rubrics can be beneficial to both students and educators. Rubrics can identify the specific gradable components of an assignment for students prior to the student beginning the assignment. A student can use rubrics to keep on track when completing an assignment. An educator can use rubrics to clearly explain the assignment objectives and expectations, provide guidelines for grading, and to provide feedback. It is important for the educator to remember that "appropriately designed rubrics can make an enormous contribution to instructional quality" (Popham, 1997, p. 75).

CHAPTER 7 APPLICATION EXERCISE

What concerns do you have regarding the use online assessment including tests/exams, self-assessment, and peer assessment? Offer suggestions for addressing your concerns.

Using the instructions provided below, develop a grading rubric for an assignment that you will use in your online course.

Instructions:

1. Determine the point value for the assignment.

2. Provide specific assignment instructions.
3. Identify at least 3 evaluative criteria and determine the point value for each criterion.
4. Develop a scoring grid that clearly identifies how each level of the evaluative criteria will be graded. The criteria you use should be different than the criteria on the sample rubric provided for you.

REFERENCES

Adams, C., & King, K. (1995). Towards a framework for student self-assessment. *Innovations In Education & Training International, 32*(4), 336–343.

Adeyemi, A. (2012). Effect of peer and self-assessment on male and female students' self-efficacy and self-autonomy in the learning of mathematics. *Gender & Behavior, 10*(1), 4492–4508.

Al–Barakat, A., & Al–Hassan, O. (2009). Peer assessment as a learning tool for enhancing student teachers' preparation. *Asia-Pacific Journal of Teacher Education, 37*(4), 399–413.

Amo, E., & Jareño, F. (2011). Self, peer, and teacher assessment as active learning methods. *Research Journal of International Studies, 18*, 41–47.

Andrade, H. (2000). Using rubrics to promote thinking and learning. *Educational Leadership, 57*(5), 13–18.

Andrade, H. (2005). Teaching with rubrics: The good, the bad, and the ugly. *College Teaching, 53(1)*, 27–30.

Andrade, H., & Du, Y. (2007). Student responses to criteria-referenced self-assessment. *Assessment & Evaluation In Higher Education, 32*(2), 159–181.

Andrade, H., & Valtcheva, A. (2009). Promoting learning and achievement through self-assessment. *Theory Into Practice, 48*, 12–19.

Andrade, H., Wang, X., Du, Y., & Akawi, R. (2009). Rubric-references self-assessment and self-efficacy for writing. *The Journal of Educational Research, 102*(4), 287–301.

Ballantyne, R., Hughes, K., & Mylonas, A. (2002). Developing procedures for using peer assessment in large classes using an action research process. *Assessment & Evaluation in Higher Education, 27*(5), 427–441. doi: 10.1080/0260293022000009302

Bloxham, S., & West, A. (2004). Understanding the rules of the game: Marking peer assessment as a medium for developing students' conceptions of assessment. *Assessment & Education In Higher Education, 29*(6), 721–733.

Bouzidi, L., & Jaillet, A. (2009). Can online peer assessment be trusted? *Educational Technology and Society, 12*(4), 257–268.

Cartney, P. (2010). Exploring the use of peer assessment as a vehicle for closing the gap between feedback given and feedback used. *Assessment & Evaluation In Higher Education, 35*(5), 551–564.

Cestone, C., Levine, R., & Lane, D. (2008). Peer assessment and evaluation in team-based learning. *New Directions For Teaching and Learning, 116*, 69–79.

Chen, Y., & Tsai, C. (2009). An educational research course facilitated by online peer assessment. *Innovations in Education and Teaching International, 46*(1), 105–117.

Davies, P. (2006). Peer assessment: Judging the quality of students' work by comments rather than marks. *Innovations in Education and Teaching International, 43*(1), 69–82.

Davis, N., Kumtepe, E., & Aydeniz, M. (2007). Fostering continuous improvement and learning through peer assessment: Part of an integral model of assessment. *Educational Assessment, 12*(2), 113–135.

De Wever, B., Van Keer, H., Schellens, T., & Valcke, M. (2009). Structuring asynchronous discussion groups: The impact of role-assignment and self-assessment on students' levels of knowledge construction through social negotiation. *Journal of Computer Assisted Learning, 25,* 177–188.

Gaytan, J., & McEwen, B. (2007). Effective online instructional and assessment strategies. *The American Journal of Distance Education, 21*(3), 117–132.

Hanrahan, S., & Isaacs, G. (2001). Assessing self- and peer-assessment: The students' views. *Higher Education Research & Development, 20*(1), 53–70.

Falchikov, N., & Goldfinch, J. (2000). Student peer assessment in higher education: A meta- analysis comparing peer and teacher marks. *Review of Educational Research, 70*(3), 287–322.

Henning, J., & Marty, M. (2008). A practical guide to implementing peer assessment in athletic training education. *Athletic Therapy Today, 13*(3), 30–33.

Hou, H., Chang, K., & Sung, Y. (2007). An analysis of peer assessment online discussions within a course that uses project-based learning. *Interactive Learning Environments, 15*(3), 237–251.

Jackson, C., & Larkin, M. (2002). Teaching students to use grading rubrics. *Teaching Exceptional Children, 35*(1), 40–45.

Joordens, S., Desa, S., & Pare, D. (2009). The pedagogical anatomy of peer assessment: Dissecting a peerscholar assignment. *Systemics, Cybernetics, and Informatics, 7*(5), 11–15.

Langan, A., Shuker, D., Cullen, W., Penny, D., Preziosi, R., & Wheater, C. (2008). Relationships between student characteristics and self-, peer, and tutor evaluations of oral presentations. *Assessment & Evaluation in Higher Education, 33*(2), 179–190.

Leonhardt, A. (2005). Using rubrics as an assessment tool in your classroom. *General Music Today, 19*(1), 10–16.

Lew, M., Alwis, W., & Schmidt, H. (2010). Accuracy of students' self-assessment and their beliefs about its utility. *Assessment and Evaluation In Higher Education, 35*(2), 135–156.

Lewis, R., Berghoff, P., & Pheeney, P. (1999). Focusing students: Three approaches for learning through evaluation. *Innovative Higher Education, 23*(3), 181–195.

Liu, N., & Carless, D. (2006). Peer feedback: The learning element of peer assessment. *Teaching in Higher Education, 11*(3), 279–290.

Macdonald, J. (2001). Exploiting online interactivity to enhance assignment development and feedback in distance education. *Open Learning, 16*(2), 179–189.

McMahon, T. (2010). Peer feedback in an undergraduate programme: Using action research to overcome students' reluctance to criticise. *Educational Action Research, 18*(2), 273–287.

Pharo, E., & de Salas, L. (2009). Implementing student peer review: Opportunity versus change management. *Journal of Geography in Higher Education, 33*(2), 199–207.

Poon, W., McNaught, C., Lam, P., & Kwan, H. (2009). Improving assessment methods in university science education with negotiated self- and peer- assessment. *Assessment In Education: Principles, Policy, & Practice, 16*(3), 331–346.

Popham, W. J. (1997). What's wrong and what's right with rubrics. *Educational Leadership, 55*(2), 72–75.

Sargeant, J., Mann, K., Van der Vleuten, C., & Metsemakers, J. (2008). Directed self-assessment: Practice and feedback within a social context. *Journal of Continuing Education In The Health Professions, 28*(1), 47–54.

Schuwirth, L., & Van Der Vleuten, C (2004). Different written assessment methods: What can be said about their strengths and weaknesses? *Medical Education, 38*(9), 974–979.

Sitthiworachart, J., & Joy, M. (2008). Computer support of effective peer assessment in an undergraduate programming class. *Journal of Computer Assisted Learning, 24*, 217–231.

Sivan, A. (2000). The implementation of peer assessment: An action research approach. *Assessment in Education, 7*(2), 193–213.

Stefl–Mabry, J. (2004). Building rubrics into powerful learning assessment tools. *Knowledge Quest, 32*(5), 21–25.

Tamjid, N., & Birjandi, P. (2011). Fostering learner autonomy through self- and peer-assessment. *International Journal of Academic Research, 3*(5), 245–251.

Taras, M. (2010). Student self-assessment: Processes and consequences. *Teaching In Higher Education, 15*(2), 199–209.

Topping, K. J. (2009). Peer assessment. *Theory Into Practice, 48*, 20–27.

Wen, M. L., & Tsai, C, C. (2006). University students' perceptions of and attitudes toward (online) peer assessment. *Higher Education, 51*(1), 27–44. doi: 10.1007/s10734-004-6375-8

Whitaker, C., Salend, S., & Duhaney, D. (2001). Creating instructional rubrics for inclusive classrooms. *Teaching Exceptional Children, 34*(2), 8–13.

Willey, K., & Gardner, A. (2010). Investigating the capacity of self and peer assessment activities to engage and promote learning. *European Journal of Engineering Education, 35*(4), 429–443.

Van den Berg, I., Admiraal, W., & Pilot, A. (2006). Design principles and outcomes of peer assessment in higher education. *Studies in Higher Education, 31*(3), 341–356.

Vickerman, P. (2009). Student perspectives on formative peer assessment: An attempt to deepen learning? *Assessment & Evaluation in Higher Education, 34*(2), 221–230.

Vu, T., & Dall'Alba, G. (2007). Students' experience of peer assessment in a professional course. *Assessment & Evaluation In Higher Education, 32*(5), 541–556.

CPSIA information can be obtained at www.ICGtesting.com
Printed in the USA
BVOW04s0020070314

346930BV00004B/29/P